NO-BAKE
Cakes & Treats

NO-BAKE
Cakes & Treats

DELECTABLE SWEETS WITHOUT TURNING ON THE OVEN

HANNAH MILES
PHOTOGRAPHY BY STEVE PAINTER

LORENZ BOOKS

Contents

Introduction

I am not going to deny that I love to bake – it is in my soul as my grandfather was a baker – but there are times when I love the simplicity of being able to rustle up something delicious for dessert or for a party treat quickly without the need to bake – this is the art of "No-Bake" cakes.

The recipes in this book do not require an oven and are made simply by heating a few ingredients in a pan or in the microwave. Some of them, such as the ice cream cakes, do not require any cooking at all! The best thing about these cakes and treats is that they can all be prepared ahead of time and stored in the refrigerator or in an airtight container or in the freezer, allowing you to get ahead before parties and friends visiting for supper, without any last-minute work needed.

Here is all you need for crispy and crunchy treats, tiffin slices, ice cream cakes, no-bake cheesecakes and showstopper no-bake centrepiece desserts.

Happy "No-Baking"!

Quick and easy desserts
that can be whipped
up in no time at all

Delicious layered desserts
that will delight
your guests

Ice cream cakes make great stand-by desserts that everyone will want to dig into with giant spoons

A rich chocolate ganache-topped strawberry cheesecake is perfect for parties

The Simple Joy Of No-Bake Cakes

I truly hope that you enjoy these make-ahead no-bake cakes and treats – all made very simply without the need for an oven. Whatever the occasion – be it fête, children's party or sophisticated dinner party – the chapters in this book offer delectable tempations for all your family and friends. The recipes are easy for children to prepare with a little adult supervision, and there are lots of hints and tips for basic techniques in the following pages to help.

The *Crispy and Crunchy Treats* chapter contains all manner of small cakes and slices – perfect for children's parties and bake sales or fêtes. They can be prepared in no time at all and are easily served in individual portions. There are classic favourites such as marshmallow crispy cakes – coloured pink and white and decorated with sugar sprinkles – chic black and white layered crispy cakes coated in milk and white chocolate and decorated with chocolate flake, or for Nutella lovers, the chocolate hazelnut squares topped with a Nutella ganache. They are always popular with my friends.

The *Fridge Cakes and Tiffin Slices* chapter contains my favourite type of no-bake cakes – rich chocolate slices bursting with biscuits, cherries and nuts. This chapter includes a chocolate peppermint slice that I used to enjoy at school, a sweet and salty after-party tiffin slice containing popcorn, pretzels and even salted crisps (you will have to trust me on this one), and a kitsch and quirky chocolate salami – which looks like its original meat counterpart until you slice into it, when biscuits and delicious green pistachio nuts are found nestling in a rich boozy chocolate ganache.

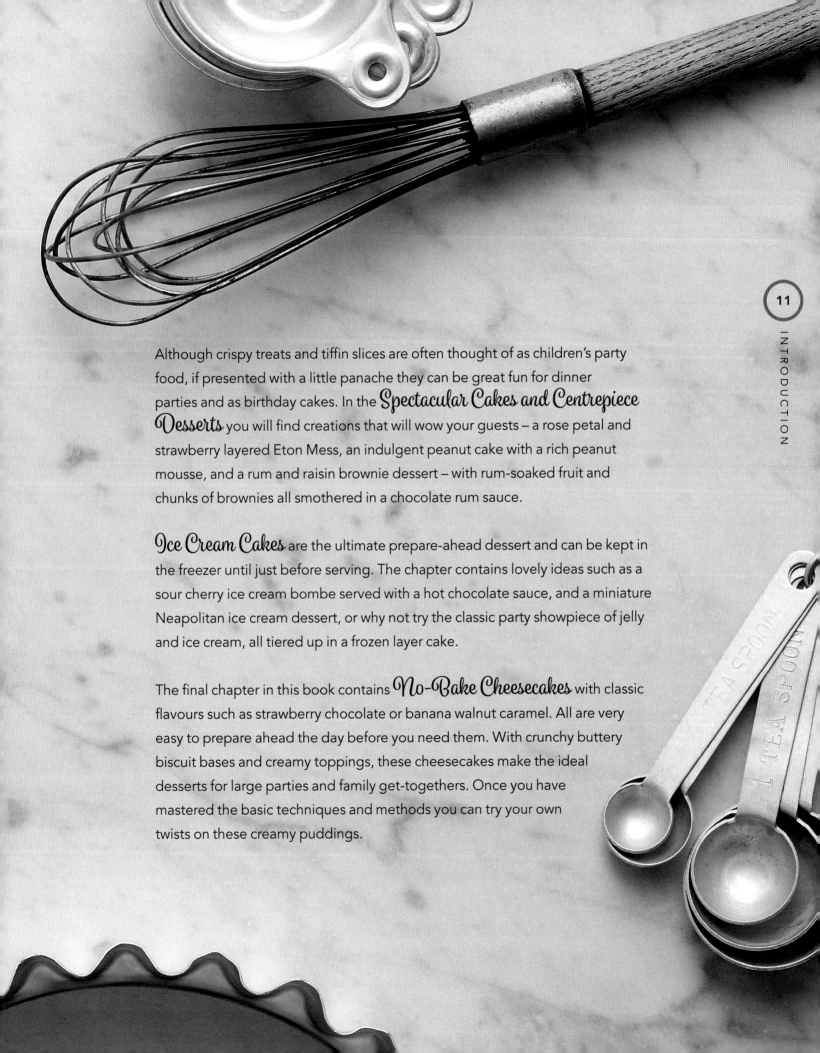

Although crispy treats and tiffin slices are often thought of as children's party food, if presented with a little panache they can be great fun for dinner parties and as birthday cakes. In the *Spectacular Cakes and Centrepiece Desserts* you will find creations that will wow your guests – a rose petal and strawberry layered Eton Mess, an indulgent peanut cake with a rich peanut mousse, and a rum and raisin brownie dessert – with rum-soaked fruit and chunks of brownies all smothered in a chocolate rum sauce.

Ice Cream Cakes are the ultimate prepare-ahead dessert and can be kept in the freezer until just before serving. The chapter contains lovely ideas such as a sour cherry ice cream bombe served with a hot chocolate sauce, and a miniature Neapolitan ice cream dessert, or why not try the classic party showpiece of jelly and ice cream, all tiered up in a frozen layer cake.

The final chapter in this book contains *No-Bake Cheesecakes* with classic flavours such as strawberry chocolate or banana walnut caramel. All are very easy to prepare ahead the day before you need them. With crunchy buttery biscuit bases and creamy toppings, these cheesecakes make the ideal desserts for large parties and family get-togethers. Once you have mastered the basic techniques and methods you can try your own twists on these creamy puddings.

Most of the ingredients in this book are simple store-cupboard items meaning that many of the recipes can be rustled up in no time without needing to rush to the shops.

To Keep in Your Store Cupboard!

CEREALS

The crispy treats chapter as well as some of the other recipes in the book use a variety of breakfast cereals. It is possible to make these recipes with almost any type of cereal and you can make some nice variations to the recipes by substituting different products – such as cinnamon grahams for a bursting cinnamon flavour – or you can use wholewheat cereals for a more healthy option. The only thing to bear in mind is that cereals have different weights and you may therefore need more or less of a substitution. It is best to judge by eye how much is needed, adding the cereal gradually and stirring well so that each flake is coated until all the syrup mixture is used up. Try to avoid using very sugary cereals, or alternatively reduce the sugar quantity in the recipe slightly.

CHOCOLATE

A lot of the recipes in this book contain chocolate, it is one of my favourite things! Chocolate is one of those ingredients where it is worth paying a little extra for good quality with a high percentage of cocoa solids as this will give a stronger and more intense chocolate flavour. With plain (semisweet) chocolate I always use at least 70% cocoa solids or for a more intense bitter chocolate flavour use 85% cocoa solid chocolate. You can vary the flavour of tiffin slices easily by using flavoured chocolate – there are all kinds available now in supermarkets, such as pistachio, orange or even spiced chilli chocolate!

BISCUITS

A wide variety of cookies are used in this book – a lot of the tiffin slices are given added crunch with chunks of biscuits or cookies, and the cheesecakes all use biscuit crumbs for their crunchy bases. The recipes call for different types of biscuits although these are no hard and fast rules and if you do not have the type that the recipe calls for you can easily substitute other plain varieties such as digestive biscuits (UK) or graham crackers (USA).

MARSHMALLOWS AND CANDIES

Marshmallows are a great sweet treat and are perfect for making crispy cakes. Melted in a pan with butter they create the most delicious gooey coating to bind together cereals. Marshmallows come in many different shapes, sizes and colours but when melted down it does not matter which variety you use. Many other sweets and candies are used in this book. If you love a particular candy, you can always substitute your favourite in the recipes instead, so feel free to experiment to create your dream sweet treat.

DAIRY PRODUCTS

The recipes in this book call for a variety of dairy products. You can use salted or unsalted butter in the recipes. If you use unsalted butter add a small pinch of salt with the butter. Delicious creams are used – crème fraîche, double (heavy) cream and clotted cream. The cheesecake chapter uses cream cheese, mascarpone cheese and ricotta cheese which are all available in supermarkets although if you have a delicatessen near you, it is worth treating yourself to their products which often taste more sumptuous. To make lighter versions, use low-fat cream cheese or low-fat crème fraîche as substitutes.

Some people shy away from baking, for fear that things can go wrong. The recipes in this book have such simple techniques that you really can't fail to create something scrumptious. Here the basic techniques are set out in individual steps that are clearly explained; once you have mastered them you can vary the flavours to suit.

Basic Techniques

The sections below explain how to melt butter and chocolate, make chocolate ganache and create perfect crispy cakes. All you need for these steps is a pan and a heatproof bowl. It's good to have a variety of sizes in your cupboard, as the recipes use different quantities of these ingredients to be melted. However, bear in mind that you may be adding large quantities of biscuit, cereal or crispies to the same pan or bowl. It is also important that any equipment you use is completely dry, so that condensation does not form whilst heating.

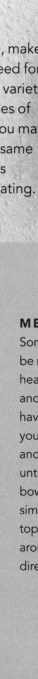

MELTING BUTTER

Some of the recipes in this book call for butter to be melted. This is best done in a pan over a gentle heat. If you use a high heat, the butter can brown and you should not use it if this happens as it will have a bitter taste. Alternatively you can chop your butter into cubes, place in a heatproof bowl and microwave on full power for 40–60 seconds until melted. Take care when removing it as the bowl and butter can be hot. If you have an Aga, simply place the butter in a heatproof bowl on top of the Aga and leave to melt. It will take around 20 minutes. Use the melted butter as directed in the recipe.

MELTING CHOCOLATE

You need to take care when melting chocolate as it can have temperamental melting properties. Break your chocolate into pieces and place the chocolate in a heatproof bowl resting over a pan of simmering water and heat until the chocolate melts. Take care that the bottom of the bowl does not touch the water and also that no water gets into the bowl as it will cause the chocolate to become grainy. Stir occasionally until all the chocolate has melted. You can use this method with plain (semisweet), milk or white chocolate.

It is also possible to melt chocolate in a heatproof bowl in the microwave, although I would not recommend doing this with white chocolate as it can easily burn. Break the chocolate into small pieces and microwave on full power for about 40–60 seconds. Stir the chocolate to melt any remaining lumps of chocolate in the heat of the melted chocolate. Use the melted chocolate as directed in the recipe.

COATING CRISPIES

Melt the quantities of marshmallows and butter called for in the recipe in a pan over a gentle heat, stirring all the time so that the marshmallows do not burn. The mixture will become very gooey as the butter and marshmallows melt and combine. Working quickly so that the marshmallow mixture does not set, stir in the cornflakes or rice crispies, adding them gradually and stirring well so that they are all coated. If the mixture seems too sticky, add more of the flakes or crispies. You want all of the flakes to be coated but not for pools of the mixture to be left in the pan. The image on the left shows the consistency to aim for.

MAKING CHOCOLATE GANACHE

This is the perfect topping for indulgent cakes and cheesecakes. To make chocolate ganache, break the chocolate into pieces and place in a heatproof bowl over a pan of simmering water with the specified quantities of cream and butter. Simmer until the chocolate and butter have melted, then stir to form a thick glossy ganache.

Alternatively, heat the broken chocolate, cream and butter on full power in the microwave for 1 minute in a heatproof bowl, stir and then heat for a further 10 seconds or so until the sauce is smooth. It is best to use good quality chocolate with a high cocoa content. If the mixture splits, stir in a little more cream or a little milk to help rescue the ganache.

BISCUIT BASES AND CASES

Biscuit or cookie bases are the ideal way to add a crunchy texture to desserts and are easy to prepare. Crush the biscuits to fine crumbs in a food processor or blender. Alternatively place them in a clear ziplock bag, seal and then bash with a rolling pin. You can wrap the bag in a dish towel to protect your work surface, if you wish. Melt the butter in a pan over the heat, cool slightly and then stir into the biscuit crumbs so that they are all coated – add the butter gradually, stirring well, so that the crumbs just come together. If the mixture is too dry add a little more melted butter. Press the crumbs into the base of the tin with the back of a spoon in an even layer.

Preparing and Lining Cake Tins

As many of the tiffin slices and cakes will need to be removed from the tins or pans before serving, it is important to line the cake tins you use carefully to make sure that your treats can be lifted out easily and don't get stuck. There are various different names for lining paper, including greaseproof, waxed, baking paper and baking parchment. Greaseproof is ideal for wrapping foods for storage. Baking parchment has a silicone lining and so is better to use when things will stick, such as meringues, but for the recipes in this book you can use any of these types of paper for lining.

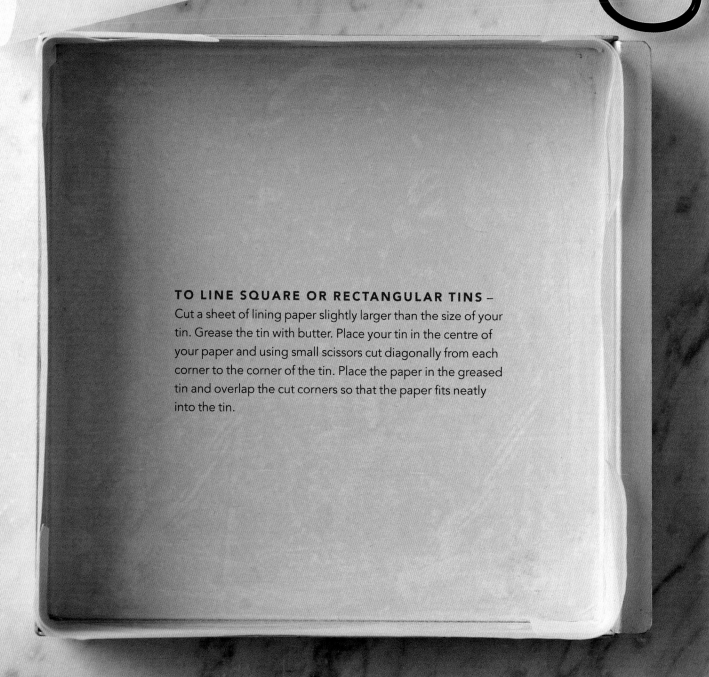

TO LINE SQUARE OR RECTANGULAR TINS – Cut a sheet of lining paper slightly larger than the size of your tin. Grease the tin with butter. Place your tin in the centre of your paper and using small scissors cut diagonally from each corner to the corner of the tin. Place the paper in the greased tin and overlap the cut corners so that the paper fits neatly into the tin.

TO LINE SANDWICH PANS – Cut a circle of lining paper the size of the base of the cake tin. Grease the pan well with butter and place the circle of paper in the bottom of the pan. You can draw around the tin to get the right size or fold the circle into eighths and trim to the right size.

TO LINE DEEP ROUND OR SQUARE TINS – Cut a long strip of lining paper slightly deeper than the tin and long enough to go round the whole tin. Fold a 3cm/1in fold along the length of the paper and snip small incisions along the fold. Cut a circle or square of lining paper the size of the bottom of the tin. Grease the tin with butter and then insert the strip of lining paper around the inside of the tin so that the snipped fringe lies flat on the bottom. Place the paper circle or square into the tin to cover the fringe.

TO LINE A BOWL OR PAN WITH CLEAR FILM – Grease the bowl or pan with a little butter or oil. Lie a large sheet of clear film or plastic wrap on a clean flat surface and then fold it in half so that you have a double layer to give added strength. Lie the sheet into the bowl or pan and smooth down flat with your hands so that it sits tightly against the sides.

Scaling Recipes

The recipes in this book can be easily scaled up or down. In order to scale down, halve the recipe ingredients and use a tin or pan smaller than that called for in the original recipe. For example, if making a tiffin slice that was originally made in a 20cm/8in square cake tin, make the half quantity in a paper-lined loaf tin instead.

You can do the same with the cheesecake and ice cream cake recipes. You will need to judge by eye whether your new tin is the right size. Take care not to overfill the tin. You can still make the cake in the original size of tin of you wish – it will just make thinner layered slices.

If you want to double the size of the recipe (for example if you are making for a large party event) double the ingredient quantity and use a tin which is approximately double the size. For example, with the cheesecake recipes you can double the quantity and make in a large roasting pan rather than the round or square cake tin listed. Make sure that the pan is greased and lined well as you will not have the benefit of a loose bottom to assist you in removing the cheesecake from a roasting pan. If you want to make even larger quantities you can quadruple the ingredients but I recommend that you make it in two larger pans as cakes larger than this will become very difficult to remove from the tin in one piece.

Problem Solving

As the cakes and treats in this book are easy and primarily just require assembly, there is very little that can go wrong. Honestly! However there are a few problem areas that you need to be aware of:

Tiffin cakes and slices getting stuck in the tin – always line the tins carefully following the instructions on pages 18–19. Before removing from the tin, slide a knife around all sides of the cake to loosen it from the tin.

Ice cream cakes are too soft – this may occur if your freezer temperature is not cold enough so just turn it up a little.

Crispy cakes are too dry or too sticky – with crispy cakes you need to judge carefully by eye as the marshmallow or

chocolate mixture that you coat the crispies or cornflake in can be slightly different each time. Always add your crispies or flakes gradually, mixing well as you go. You want all the crispies to be coated and for there not to be too much of the chocolate or marshmallow mixture loose in the pan. If the mixture is too gooey add more crispies, a handful at a time.

Cheesecakes are not set – leave it for longer in the refrigerator and it should set. If you are making a gelatine cheesecake and it doesn't set the only option (and it is not an ideal one) is to put the cheesecake topping back into a bowl. Clean the tin as much as possible, leaving the biscuit or cookie base in place. Melt another leaf of gelatine or two in a little hot water then mix into the cheesecake mixture. Pour back into the tin and chill in the refrigerator.

Storage

I have to confess that the storage time for the recipes in this book does not normally get tested as the cakes are usually gone as soon as they are served! That said, they do keep well. The crispy treats, such as rice crispy cakes, will store for up to three days in an airtight container or on a plate wrapped in clear film or plastic wrap. Any cakes which are chilled or set in the refrigerator should be stored in the refrigerator wrapped in clear film and will keep for up to three days in this way.

This includes the tiffin cakes, cheesecakes and many of the desserts in this book. Ice cream cakes can be stored in the freezer for up to a month.

Any cakes served with fresh whipped cream or clotted cream need to be eaten on the day they are made as they do not keep. Storage instructions for specific recipes are given at the end of each recipe.

Packaging and Gifts

I love nothing more than packaging sweet treats for gifts. Whilst there are plenty of nice cakes to buy in the shop, nothing is more personal than saying thank you with a homemade present. It really shows you have taken the time to create something special yourself. There are a wide variety of gift bags and cake boxes available nowadays. I like to save wicker baskets and line them with pretty tissue and then fill with small cakes. Wrapped up in cellophane and tied with a bow they make the perfect hostess gift. For an extra-special present why not buy your friend a cake stand and then make one of the larger cakes in this book and present it on the stand wrapped in cellophane.

If you are hosting a cake stall at a fête many of the small and large cakes are perfect for wrapping up and selling. Wrapping tiffin slices in lining paper tied up with red and white bakers twine looks very attractive. You can decorate these with pretty stickers and gift tags letting the recipient know what is inside. To package individual slices of cheesecake, carefully cut the cheesecake into slices and place them individually on paper plates. You can then wrap the slices in clear film and then tie them with ribbons.

Ice cream cakes are, I have to admit, practically impossible to gift package as they start to melt almost immediately. It is therefore best to serve these at home!

Icebox Cakes

There is a real trend at the moment for icebox cakes. They are one of my favourite types of cakes as they can be prepared well in advance of being needed and just stored in the freezer. It is important to line your tin, pan or bowl to make sure you can remove it easily before serving.

The easiest way to make an icebox cake is to line the base and sides of a tin with biscuit or cookie crumb base mixed with butter. Once set this will hold your ice cream in a perfect shape. You can use any flavour of ice cream that you like – chocolate, mint chip or salted caramel or even low-fat frozen yogurt if you are watching the calories.

You can serve your icebox cake simply, just with a warm chocolate or caramel sauce to drizzle over, but if you want a

more spectacular centrepiece, decorate with chocolate candies, toasted marshmallows or sweet fruit compote.

Remove your icebox cake from the freezer about 5–10 minutes before serving, depending on how warm your kitchen is, so that it is soft enough to cut into slices.

Crispy and Crunchy Treats

This chapter is full of tiny sweet treats that are perfect for fêtes and bake sales, kid's parties or lunchboxes. The recipes are simple and with a little adult supervision are fine for children to make themselves. All your best-loved crispy cakes are included – peanut butter, chocolate hazelnut and classic chocolate Easter nests.

For slightly more unusual flavours why not try the coconut popping candy cakes or the malted cornflake cakes, infused with malt powder and crushed chocolate malt balls. One of my favourite recipes is the ever-popular salted caramel – rich butter, salted toffee, coated cornflakes – great with a cup of tea or coffee for elevenses.

For parties there are pretty pink and white crispy cakes decorated with sugar sprinkles – just right for party princesses – or for a more grown-up two-tone treat, try the dark and white crispy slices, coated in milk and white chocolate and topped with crumbled chocolate flake.

Crispy cakes bring out the inner child in everyone

Shards of delicious
hazelnut praline make
pretty decorations

A few drops of food
colouring create
spectacular rainbow effects

These crispy squares are super sweet and salty – rich with peanut butter and white chocolate, they are a very yummy treat. If you can't find honey-roasted cashews then you can happily substitute with honey-roasted peanuts instead.

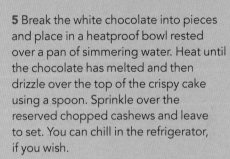

Peanut Butter and Cashew Squares

MAKES 24 SQUARES
PREPARATION TIME 20 MINUTES,
PLUS SETTING

150g/5oz honey-roasted cashew nuts
300g/10oz/7–8 cups marshmallows
125g/4½oz/9 tbsp butter
150g/5oz peanut butter
200g/7oz/7 cups rice crispies
200g/7oz white chocolate

Equipment: 30 x 20cm/12 x 8in tin or pan, greased and lined; 24 cake cases

1 Roughly chop the cashew nuts on a chopping board. Set aside until needed.

2 In a large heavy pan, melt the marshmallows and butter over a gentle heat, stirring all the time so that the marshmallows do not burn. The mixture will become very gooey. Stir in the peanut butter and mix in well.

3 Working quickly so that the marshmallow mixture does not cool, stir in the rice crispies and half of the chopped cashews (reserving the remainder for the topping) and stir well so that everything is coated.

4 Spoon the mixture into the prepared tin and press down with the back of a spoon.

5 Break the white chocolate into pieces and place in a heatproof bowl rested over a pan of simmering water. Heat until the chocolate has melted and then drizzle over the top of the crispy cake using a spoon. Sprinkle over the reserved chopped cashews and leave to set. You can chill in the refrigerator, if you wish.

6 Once the chocolate has set, cut the cake into 24 squares and place in cake cases to serve. These cakes will store for up to 3 days in an airtight container.

For an almond version of these cakes, replace the peanut butter with almond butter and the honey-roasted cashew nuts with honey-roasted almonds instead.

These pink and white cakes are perfect for any little girl's princess party. You can colour the marshmallow the colour of your choice of course – so for a space party why not try bright green and purple and top with multi-coloured sugar sprinkles. You can also replace the rice crispies with another plain breakfast cereal if you wish.

Pink and White Marshmallow Crispy Cakes

MAKES 14
PREPARATION TIME 15 MINUTES,
PLUS COOLING

340g/12oz/8–9 cups marshmallows
125g/4½oz/9 tbsp butter
A few drops of pink food colouring
170g/6oz/6 cups rice crispies
Sugar sprinkles

Equipment: 2 x muffin tins or pans;
*   14 muffin cases*

1 Place the 14 muffin cases in the muffin tins.

2 In a large heavy pan, melt the marshmallows and butter over a gentle heat, stirring all the time so that the marshmallows do not burn. The mixture will become very gooey.

3 Divide the marshmallow mixture between two bowls and add a few drops of pink food colouring to one of the bowls. Working quickly so that the mixture does not cool, stir half of the rice crispies into each bowl and stir well so that all the crispies are coated. You can leave half of the marshmallow mixture in the pan and stir it there to save on washing up, if you wish.

4 Place alternating spoonfuls of crispies into the cases so that they are layered with pink and white stripes. Top with sugar sprinkles and leave to cool before serving. These cakes will store for up to 3 days in an airtight container.

These crispy treats are perfect for a black and white themed party. You can also make them as rainbow-coloured slices by adding a few drops of food colouring to the marshmallow mixture, omitting the plain and milk chocolate, and then create coloured layers in your tin. If you want to make a smaller quantity, simply halve the recipe ingredients.

Black and White Rice Crispy Slices

MAKES 32
PREPARATION TIME 30 MINUTES, PLUS CHILLING

400g/14oz/10 cups marshmallows
100g/3½oz/7 tbsp butter
300g/10½oz white chocolate
200g/7oz/7 cups rice crispies
150g/5oz plain (semisweet) chocolate
200g/7oz milk chocolate
Chocolate flake, to decorate

Equipment: 20cm/8in square loose-bottomed tin or pan, greased and lined; cooling rack; foil or lining paper; baking sheet

1 Place half of the marshmallows and half of the butter in a pan and heat over a gentle heat until melted. Break 100g/3½oz of the white chocolate into pieces and add to the warm marshmallow mixture and stir until the chocolate has melted.

2 Add half of the rice crispies to the bowl and stir well so that all the crispies are coated in the marshmallow mixture. Tip the mixture into the lined tin and press down with the back of a spoon to a flat level.

3 In a second pan, heat the remaining marshmallows and butter over a gentle heat until melted. Add the plain chocolate broken into pieces and stir until the chocolate melts. Add the

remaining rice crispies and stir well until they are all coated.

4 Press the dark chocolate crispies on top of the white chocolate crispies pressing down with the back of a spoon. Chill in the refrigerator for at least 2 hours until set.

5 Place the milk chocolate broken into pieces into a heatproof bowl resting over a pan of simmering water and do the same with the remaining white chocolate. Simmer both until melted and then remove from the heat and allow the chocolate to cool. You want the chocolate to cool but not set as it still needs to be runny to be spread over the crispy slices.

6 Remove the rice crispy cake from the pan, leaving it on the bottom metal layer of the tin, and cut into 4 equal rectangles.

7 Place the slices on a cooling rack with a sheet of foil or lining paper underneath to catch any chocolate drips. Spread the white chocolate over the top sides and ends of two of the slices. Repeat with the milk chocolate over the two remaining slices.

8 Sprinkle with crushed chocolate flake to decorate. Place the slices carefully on a baking sheet and chill in the refrigerator for an hour until the chocolate has set. Cut the rectangles into slices to serve. They will store in the refrigerator for at least 3 days.

Salted caramel is one of those recent food trends so yummy that it makes you question why someone didn't discover it sooner. These classic crispy cakes have a delicious salted caramel flavour – they are one of my favourites.

Salted Caramel Cornflake Cakes

MAKES 15
PREPARATION TIME 20 MINUTES, PLUS COOLING

100g/3½oz/½ cup caster (superfine) sugar
200g/7oz/1 stick and 6 tbsp butter
A pinch of sea salt flakes
300g/10oz/7–8 cups marshmallows
200g/7oz/6–7 cups cornflakes

Equipment: 2 x muffin tins or pans;
 15 muffin cases

1 In a pan, heat the sugar and butter until the sugar has melted, then continue to heat, stirring all the time until the mixture starts to caramelize and goes golden brown. You want the caramel to be a deep golden brown colour but take care that the mixture does not overcook and burn.

2 Add the salt to the pan with the marshmallows and stir the mixture over a gentle heat until all the marshmallows have melted.

3 Stir in the cornflakes and toss well in the salted caramel mixture so that each flake is coated.

4 Place 15 cake cases in muffin tins and place a large spoonful of mixture in each, piling each one high above the tops. Leave to cool for about 30 minutes then store in an airtight container for up to 3 days.

You can add salt to your own taste – start with a pinch and add a little more if you want a real salty kick.

For those of you who love the flavour of malt then these are the crispy cakes for you – they are made with malted milk drinking powder and chocolate malt balls which give a delicious malty taste. These cakes are perfect for a midnight feast! You can make them with any cereal of your choosing – rice crispies or shredded wheat cereal also work well. If you prefer plain chocolate to milk chocolate this is also an easy substitution.

Malted Chocolate Crispy Cakes

MAKES 20
PREPARATION TIME 15 MINUTES,
PLUS COOLING

125ml/4fl oz/½ cup golden (light corn) syrup
50g/1¾oz/3½ tbsp butter
85g/3oz/½ cup malted milk drinking powder, such as Horlicks
100g/3½oz milk chocolate
130g/4½oz/1½ cups chocolate malt balls, such as Maltesers
200g/7oz cornflakes or other unsweetened cereal

Equipment: 2 x muffin tins or pans; 20 muffin cases

These are sophisticated versions of the crispy children's party treats.

1 Place the 20 muffin cases in the muffin tins.

2 In a pan heat the golden syrup and butter over a gentle heat until the butter has melted. Stir in the malted powder and mix well so that it is all incorporated.

3 Break the chocolate into pieces and add to the pan and stir until the chocolate has melted. The chocolate will melt in the heat of the caramel.

4 Chop the chocolate malt balls into pieces using a sharp knife. Add most of the malt balls to the mixture with the cornflakes, reserving some to sprinkle on top for decoration. Stir well so that all the cereal is coated in the chocolate.

5 Place spoonfuls of crispies into the cases so that they are filled generously.

6 Sprinkle over the reserved chopped chocolate malt balls to decorate and leave to cool before serving. If you do this whilst the crispy mixture is still warm, the chocolate on the malt balls will melt and fix them in place when the cakes cool. These cakes will store for up to 3 days in an airtight container.

I love to make homemade chocolate hazelnut spread – it is great smeared thickly on buttered toast. These scrumptious crispy squares are perfect for anyone who loves Nutella as they are topped with a generous chocolate layer of hazelnut ganache.

Hazelnut Praline Squares

MAKES 16 SQUARES
PREPARATION TIME 30 MINUTES,
PLUS SETTING

FOR THE PRALINE
50g/1¾oz/¼ cup caster (superfine) sugar
50g/1¾oz/½ cup blanched hazelnuts

FOR THE CARAMEL
15ml/1 tbsp golden (light corn) syrup
15ml/1 tbsp glucose
100g/3½oz/2½–3 cups marshmallows
80g/2¾oz/5½ tbsp butter
120g/4oz/4 cups rice crispies
50g/1¾oz/⅓ cup chopped roasted
    hazelnuts

FOR THE TOPPING
100g/3½oz plain (semisweet) chocolate
15ml/1 tbsp butter
30ml/2 tbsp chocolate hazelnut spread,
    such as Nutella
40g/1⅓oz/2 tbsp chopped roasted
    hazelnuts

*Equipment: silicone mat or greased baking
    sheet; food processor or blender;
    20cm/8in square tin or pan, greased
    and lined*

*If you do not have time
to make the hazelnut
praline you can just add
the finely chopped
hazelnuts instead.*

1 Begin by preparing the hazelnut praline. Heat the sugar in a pan until melted. Do not stir the pan as the sugar is cooking but swirl it to ensure that the sugar does not burn. Cook until the caramel is golden brown in colour. Spread the hazelnuts out on a silicone mat or greased baking sheet and carefully pour over the caramel. Leave to cool and then blitz in a food processor or blender to very fine crumbs.

2 For the caramel, place the golden syrup, glucose, marshmallows and butter in a pan and heat gently until the butter and marshmallows have melted. Stir in the hazelnut praline powder and mix well. Add the rice crispies and chopped hazelnuts and stir so that they are coated in the mixture.

3 Spoon the mixture into the tin and press out with the back of a spoon into an even layer. Leave to cool.

4 Place a heatproof bowl over a pan of simmering water and add the plain chocolate broken into pieces, and then the butter. Stir until melted and the chocolate and butter are fully combined. Add the chocolate hazelnut spread and stir in well. The mixture will thicken.

5 Spread the chocolate mixture over the top of the crispy cake and sprinkle with the chopped hazelnuts. Leave in the refrigerator to set for 3 hours then cut into 16 squares and serve. This will store in an airtight container for up to 3 days.

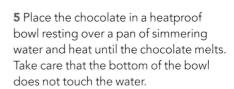

I love coconut – it is one of my favourite ingredients. I use long shredded sweetened coconut which is delicious but if you cannot find this you can use coconut shavings or desiccated coconut instead. Put the popping candy on just before serving for maximum "popping" effect.

Coconut Popping Candy Cakes

MAKES 24
PREPARATION TIME 15 MINUTES, PLUS COOLING

150g/5oz/1⅔ cups shredded coconut
250ml/8fl oz/1 cup coconut cream
50g/1¾oz/¼ cup caster (superfine) sugar
300g/10oz/8 cups marshmallows
85g/3oz/5½ tbsp butter
225g/7oz/7 cups rice crispies
100g/3½oz plain (semisweet) chocolate
30ml/2 tbsp popping candy (optional)

Equipment: 2 x muffin tins or pans;
* 24 muffin cases*

1 Place the 24 muffin cases in the muffin tins.

2 Toast the coconut in a dry frying pan until light golden brown. Watch carefully as it can burn easily. When it is a light golden brown, tip out on to a plate. Do not leave in the pan as it will continue to cook in the heat and can burn.

3 In a large pan, heat the coconut cream and sugar for about 5 minutes until thick and syrupy. Add the marshmallows and butter to the pan over a gentle heat, stirring all the time so that the marshmallows do not burn. The mixture will become very gooey.

4 Working quickly so that the marshmallow mixture does not set, stir in the rice crispies and three quarters of the toasted coconut and mix well so that all the crispies are coated. Divide the mixture between the muffin cases.

5 Place the chocolate in a heatproof bowl resting over a pan of simmering water and heat until the chocolate melts. Take care that the bottom of the bowl does not touch the water.

6 Drizzle the chocolate over the top of the cakes with a fork in thin lines, then sprinkle with the remaining toasted coconut. Leave to set before serving. Just before serving, sprinkle with the popping candy, if using.

These little treats are also perfect to rustle up quickly for a children's birthday party.

These little caramel nests are a classic Easter treat. I remember making them in school cooking lessons many years ago. You can fill them with any mini eggs you like, I used mini eggs but foil-covered eggs would also look pretty, just placing one or two inside each nest. If you want, you can make mini nests in a mini muffin tin instead, for tiny mouthfuls.

Caramel Crispy Nests

MAKES 12
PREPARATION TIME 20 MINUTES

300g/10oz chocolate-covered nougat and
   caramel bars, such as Mars (6 bars)
160g/5¾oz/1 stick and 3 tbsp butter
5ml/1 tsp vanilla extract
100g/3½oz milk chocolate
180g/6½oz shredded wheat cereal
100g/3½oz mini sugar eggs (36 eggs)

Equipment: 12-hole muffin tin or pan;
   12 muffin cases

1 Cut the bars into pieces and place with the butter and vanilla in a large bowl over a pan of simmering water. Stir occasionally until the butter and bars have melted. Add the milk chocolate and stir until the chocolate melts and the mixture thickens and combines.

2 Crush the shredded wheat cereal into small pieces and stir into the chocolate caramel mixture.

3 Place the muffin cases into the tin and spoon the mixture into the cases. Press an indent into the middle of each nest with the back of a spoon and place a few sugar eggs in the centre of each nest. Leave to cool before serving. These cakes will store for up to 3 days in an airtight container.

These cakes are just the thing for a springtime party – you could even use them as place name markers on your festive table.

Fridge Cakes and Tiffin Slices

I have loved chocolate tiffin ever since I was young. My Auntie Jane used to make us a chocolate tiffin Christmas pudding every year and it was one of the highlights of Christmas – rich chocolate ganache filled with cherries, biscuits and fruits and topped with glacé icing. Our family recipe for this festive treat is included in this chapter.

Tiffin cakes are ideal as they store well in the refrigerator and can just be cut into slices when you want to serve them. In addition to the classic chocolate tiffin recipe, in this version topped with garden decorations and Oreo crumbs to look like mud, the chapter contains an indulgent black forest cherry slice, inspired by my many travels to Germany, and a chocolate "salami", popular in Italy.

For a more quirky treat, why not try the "After-Party" tiffin – a sweet and salty combination of chocolate ganache, salty crisps and sweet popcorn. You will have to trust me that despite the inclusion of some unexpected ingredients, this is very yummy!

Chocolate peppermint slice is a childhood favourite

Tiffin slices are great for fêtes and parties

Crunchy biscuits and nuts enrobed in rich chocolate ganache

A chocolate tiffin Christmas pudding makes the perfect festive treat

Inspired by compost cookies that I ate in Momofuku bakery in New York, this is a chocolate slice with a difference. It has the perfect combination of saltiness from the crisps and pretzels and sweetness from the chocolate and syrup. I call them my "after-party" treats as they are great for using up leftover crisps, pretzels and popcorn!

Sweet and Salty After-party Tiffin

MAKES 25
PREPARATION TIME 20 MINUTES, PLUS CHILLING

400g/14oz plain (semisweet) chocolate
100g/3½oz golden (light corn) syrup
200g/7oz/1 stick and 6 tbsp butter
100g/3½oz salted pretzels
45g/1½oz sweet and salty popcorn
75g/2⅔oz ready salted crisps (US potato chips)

Equipment: 25cm/10in square loose-bottomed cake tin or pan, greased and lined; 25 cake cases

1 Break the chocolate into squares and place in a large heatproof bowl with the syrup and butter over a pan of simmering water. Simmer, stirring, until the chocolate melts and the mixture becomes smooth and glossy.

2 Stir in the pretzels, popcorn and crisps and mix well so that they are all coated in the chocolate mixture.

3 Spoon the mixture into the cake tin and press down level. Leave to chill in the refrigerator for at least 3 hours.

4 Cut into squares and place in the cake cases to serve. These squares will store in the refrigerator for up to 3 days.

If you have not discovered S'mores – then I urge you to do so! They are the perfect campfire treat – toasted marshmallows and chocolate sandwiched between graham crackers (similar to the humble digestive). The warm marshmallow melts the chocolate making this one indulgent and happiness-inducing mouthful. This is my no-bake version – no campfire necessary!

S'mores Bites

MAKES 16
PREPARATION TIME 30 MINUTES,
PLUS CHILLING

200g/7oz plain (semisweet) chocolate
100g/3½oz/7 tbsp butter
30ml/2 tbsp golden (light corn) syrup
Pinch of vanilla salt or regular salt
130g/4½oz digestive biscuits or graham
   crackers
75g/2⅔oz/about 2 cups marshmallows
   or mini marshmallows, chopped, plus
   8 marshmallows for the topping

*Equipment: 20cm/8in square loose-
bottomed cake tin or pan, greased and
lined; chef's blow torch; 16 cake cases*

1 Break the chocolate into squares and place in a heatproof bowl with the butter, golden syrup and salt over a pan of simmering water. Simmer, stirring, until the chocolate melts and the mixture becomes smooth and glossy.

2 Break the digestives into small pieces and stir into the chocolate mixture. Cut the marshmallows or mini marshmallows into pieces and stir into the chocolate as well. Spoon the mixture into the prepared tin, spread in an even layer and leave to chill in the refrigerator for at least 3 hours.

3 Cut the 8 topping marshmallows in half horizontally and toast each with a chef's blow torch until lightly caramelized. Cut the cake into 16 squares and place each one in a cake case. Top each cake with half a toasted marshmallow to serve.

These little cakes are topped with chocolate "mud" and with piped leaves and sugar flowers they look just like a slice of garden (they were inspired by my friend Lesley). The cake contains chocolate-coated raisins and Minstrels (chocolate discs in hard glazed sugar shells) but you can substitute other dried fruit such as blueberries or cranberries and chocolate-coated candy beans, such as Smarties or M&M's, if you like.

Oreo Cookie Garden Cakes

MAKES 16
PREPARATION TIME 30 MINUTES, PLUS CHILLING TIME

300g/10oz Oreo or similar chocolate cookies
350g/12½oz plain (semisweet) chocolate
100g/3½oz golden (light corn) syrup
175g/6¼oz/1 stick and 3½ tbsp butter
100g/3½oz chocolate-coated raisins
150g/5oz hard chocolate-coated candy beans, such as Minstrels

FOR THE DECORATION
60ml/4 tbsp ready-made buttercream icing or frosting
A few drops of green food colouring
16 sugar flowers

Equipment: food processor or blender; 20cm/ 8in square loose-bottomed cake tin or pan, greased and lined; 16 cake cases; piping or pastry bag fitted with a leaf nozzle

1 Blitz 75g/3oz of the Oreo cookies in a food processor or blender to make chocolate "mud", and set aside.

2 Break the chocolate into squares and place in a heatproof bowl with the syrup and butter over a pan of simmering water. Simmer until the chocolate melts and the mixture becomes smooth and glossy, stirring occasionally. Leave to cool.

3 Break the remaining Oreo cookies into small pieces with your hands and stir into the chocolate mixture with the raisins and candy beans.

4 Spoon the mixture into the cake tin and press down to level using the back of a spoon. Sprinkle over the reserved chocolate mud, making sure that the whole cake is covered. Leave to chill in the refrigerator for at least 3 hours.

5 Remove from the refrigerator and cut into 16 squares. Place each one in a cake case.

6 Colour the buttercream green with a few drops of food colouring and spoon into the piping bag fitted with the leaf nozzle. Pipe a green leaf on top of each square. Place a sugar flower at the edge of each leaf. These cakes will store in the refrigerator for up to 3 days.

To save time, rather than piping leaves use sugar flowers with leaves already attached.

Germany is one of my favourite holiday destinations and this chocolate cherry slice is inspired by the delicious Schwarzwald chocolate cake I love to eat when travelling there. If you want to be super-indulgent, you can decorate the top of each square with a chocolate-dipped cherry as well. The squares are very rich so you only need to serve in small portions. If you are making it for children omit the Kirsch.

Black Forest Slice

MAKES 30
PREPARATION TIME 20 MINUTES, PLUS CHILLING

400g/14oz plain (semisweet) chocolate
100g/3½oz golden (light corn) syrup
200g/7oz/1 stick and 6 tbsp butter
30ml/2 tbsp Kirsch (optional)
400g/14oz chocolate digestive biscuits (graham crackers), broken into pieces
400g/14oz/1½ cups morello cherry compote

Equipment: 25cm/10in square loose-bottomed cake tin or pan, greased and lined; 30 cake cases

1 Break the chocolate into squares and place in a heatproof bowl with the syrup and butter over a pan of simmering water. Simmer until the chocolate melts and the mixture becomes smooth and glossy, stirring occasionally.

2 Stir in the Kirsch, if using, chocolate digestive pieces and cherry compote, and stir well so that everything is coated in the chocolate mixture.

3 Spoon the mixture into the cake tin and press down to level with the back of a spoon. Leave to chill in the refrigerator for at least 3 hours.

4 Cut the square into 3 equal rectangles then cut each into 10 thin slices and place in the cake cases to serve. These cakes will store in the refrigerator for up to 3 days.

When I was at school, occasionally these delicious chocolate mint slices would be served as dessert – they were my favourite days. Although the slice has three separate layers, they do not take long to prepare. With rich chocolate ganache on top and mint green frosting, these slices look very indulgent. They make a great treat for picnics.

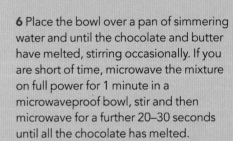

Chocolate Peppermint Slice

MAKES ABOUT 20
PREPARATION TIME 20 MINUTES,
PLUS SETTING

FOR THE BASE
300g/10oz chocolate digestive biscuits (graham crackers)
100g/3½oz/7 tbsp butter, plus extra for greasing

FOR THE PEPPERMINT LAYER
200g/7oz/1½ cups icing (confectioners') sugar, sifted
50g/1¾oz/3½ tbsp butter, softened
15ml/1 tbsp milk
5ml/1 tsp peppermint extract
A few drops of green food colouring

FOR THE GANACHE TOPPING
200g/7oz plain (semisweet) chocolate (preferably 70% cocoa solids)
80ml/5½ tbsp double (heavy) cream
15g/½oz/1 tbsp butter, melted
15ml/1 tbsp golden (light corn) syrup

Equipment: food processor or blender; 35 x 12cm/14 x 4½in rectangular loose-bottomed cake tin or pan, greased and lined; about 20 cake cases

1 Blitz the biscuits to fine crumbs in a food processor or blender. Melt the butter and then stir into the crumbs so that they are all coated. The chocolate will start to melt.

2 Spoon the crumbs into the prepared cake tin and press down in an even layer over the base using the back of a spoon. Transfer to the refrigerator to set.

3 For the peppermint layer, in a separate bowl, cream together the icing sugar, butter, milk and a few drops of the peppermint extract and green food colouring to make a smooth, thick icing. Whisk for a few minutes until the icing is light and creamy.

4 Remove the tin from the refrigerator and spread the icing over the biscuit base. Return the tin to the refrigerator for an hour to set. It is important to let the icing set before putting the ganache on top.

5 To prepare the ganache, break the chocolate into pieces into a heatproof bowl and add the cream and butter.

6 Place the bowl over a pan of simmering water and until the chocolate and butter have melted, stirring occasionally. If you are short of time, microwave the mixture on full power for 1 minute in a microwaveproof bowl, stir and then microwave for a further 20–30 seconds until all the chocolate has melted.

7 Stir the mixture until you have a thick, glossy sauce and stir in the golden syrup. Leave the mixture to cool for a few minutes then spread over the top of the peppermint icing.

8 Chill in the refrigerator for 2–3 hours until the ganache has set. Cut the cake into small slices and place in cake cases to serve. They will keep for up to 3 days stored in the refrigerator.

If you don't like mint, replace the peppermint extract with vanilla for a vanilla cream slice.

Stem ginger is a delicious tangy baking ingredient – just a small amount gives such a piquant flavour. These tiffin squares are made with two types of ginger biscuits – ginger snaps in the base and buttery brandy snaps on top – perfect for afternoon tea or as after-dinner petits fours.

Ginger Truffle Squares

MAKES 16
PREPARATION TIME 20 MINUTES,
PLUS SETTING

FOR THE BASE
250g/9oz ginger snap biscuits (cookies)
100g/3½oz/7 tbsp butter

FOR THE GANACHE
200g/7oz plain (semisweet) chocolate
100g/3½oz/7 tbsp butter
125ml/4fl oz/½ cup crème fraîche
140g/4½oz/2 tbsp chopped stem ginger
    preserved in syrup

FOR THE TOPPING
100g/3½oz brandy snaps, crushed

Equipment: food processor or blender;
20cm/8in square loose bottom cake tin or
pan, greased and lined; 16 cake cases

1 Blitz the ginger snap biscuits to fine crumbs in a food processor or blender. Melt the butter and then stir into the crumbs so that they are all coated.

2 Spoon the crumbs into the prepared cake tin and press down in an even layer over the base using the back of a spoon. Transfer to the refrigerator to set for at least 30 minutes.

3 Break the chocolate into squares and place in a heatproof bowl with the butter and crème fraîche over a pan of simmering water. Simmer until the chocolate melts and the mixture becomes smooth and glossy, stirring occasionally.

4 Stir in the finely chopped ginger with a tablespoon of the preserving syrup. Spoon the mixture into the tin on top of the biscuit base.

5 Crush the brandy snaps into small pieces and sprinkle over the chocolate ganache. Leave to set in the refrigerator for at least 3 hours.

6 Cut into squares and place in the cake cases to serve. These ginger squares will store in the refrigerator for up to 3 days.

Festive brandy snaps give this cake a pretty lace-effect topping.

When we were little, every Christmas my Auntie Jane would make a "kids" Christmas pudding – in those days we weren't too keen on traditional Christmas pudding so this used to be our version. I still make it every year at Christmas even though I am a grown-up – the brandy is just for adults! With cinnamon and ginger spices and topped with a rich glacé icing, holly and red chocolate candies, this is a great little festive treat.

Christmas Pudding Tiffin

SERVES 14
PREPARATION TIME 20 MINUTES,
PLUS CHILLING

200g/7oz plain (semisweet) chocolate
180g/6½oz/1 stick and 4½ tbsp butter
45ml/3 tbsp golden (light corn) syrup
170g/6oz ginger biscuits
170g/6oz Oreo cookies or similar chocolate
  cookies
115g/4oz/1 cup raisins, jumbo if available
60g/2oz/½ cup glacé cherries, halved
10ml/2 tsp ground cinnamon
30ml/2 tbsp brandy

TO DECORATE
150g/5oz/1 generous cup fondant icing
  (confectioners') sugar, sifted
2 red chocolate-coated candies
Sprig of holly

Equipment: 1 pudding basin or heatproof
* bowl, greased*

1 Place the chocolate, butter and syrup in a bowl over a pan of simmering water and stir until melted. Crush the ginger biscuits and Oreo cookies into small pieces and mix into the chocolate mixture with the raisins, cherries, cinnamon and brandy.

2 Spoon the mixture into the pudding basin or heatproof bowl and leave to set in the refrigerator overnight.

3 When you are ready to serve, slide a knife around the edge of the basin and turn out on to a serving plate.

4 Mix the icing sugar with about 15ml/1 tbsp of water until you have a very thick icing. Pour the icing over the top of the pudding, letting it run a little down the sides to look like a Christmas pudding, and decorate with the red chocolate candies and the holly.

5 Wrap a little clear film, plastic wrap or foil around the stem of the holly before inserting it into the cake. Cut into slices to serve. This cake will store for up to 5 days in the refrigerator.

If you are feeling creative make sugar paste holly leaves to top the pudding. If using fresh holly make sure it is wiped clean.

Do not worry that this slice contains any meat! It is in fact a classic Italian treat that is just designed to play a trick and look like salami until you cut it. By wrapping the ganache mixture in clear film and leaving it to set, the outside of the roll gets a crinkled pattern, and when dusted in a layer of icing sugar it looks like a traditional salami. If you are giving it as a gift, you can decorate the outside with printed salami labels easily found online. Omit the liqueur if serving for children.

Salame di Cioccolato

**MAKES 1 LARGE SALAMI/20 SLICES
PREPARATION TIME 20 MINUTES,
PLUS CHILLING**

225g/8oz plain (semisweet) chocolate
125g/4oz/1 stick butter
2 egg yolks
Pinch of coffee salt (or regular sea salt)
30ml/2 tbsp coffee liqueur
100g/3½oz/¾ cup pistachio nuts
100g/3½oz rich tea or other plain vanilla
    biscuits (cookies)
15ml/1 tbsp icing (confectioners') sugar
    plus extra for dusting

*Equipment: clear film or plastic wrap;
    greaseproof paper*

1 Break the chocolate into small pieces and place with the butter in a heatproof bowl over a pan of simmering water and heat until melted. Remove the bowl from the heat and beat in the egg yolks, whisking well. Stir in the coffee salt and liqueur together with the pistachio nuts.

2 Break the biscuits into small pieces and stir in together with the tablespoon of icing sugar. Leave to cool until the mixture becomes thick.

3 Once the mixture has thickened, place it on to a double layer sheet of clear film and roll into a sausage shape, twisting the ends of the clear film tightly. Leave to set in the refrigerator.

4 After 30 minutes, remove the slice from the refrigerator and roll it, still in its clear film, on a clean kitchen surface to make a perfect sausage shape (as it will have lost its shape slightly as the mixture sets), then return to the refrigerator.

5 When you are ready to serve, remove the clear film, dust a large sheet of greaseproof paper with icing sugar and roll the salami on it to coat, to give it a salami-looking effect.

6 Store in the refrigerator for up to 5 days in an airtight container or wrapped in clear film. It is pretty presented in a wrapping of greaseproof paper, tied with butcher's twine.

Spectacular Cakes and Centrepiece Desserts

Although no-bake cakes are quick and easy to prepare this does not mean that they don't deserve a place at a dinner party – after all everyone loves crispy cakes and tiffin so why not give your guests happy childhood memories by serving one of these delicious desserts.

The recipes in this chapter are all perfect for suppers and parties as they need to be prepared ahead and are then ready to be served just when you need them. There is a delectable cinnamon pretzel cake, layered with cinnamon and chocolate mousses, irresistible salty pretzels, and a pretty blueberry and white chocolate layer dessert, made with a flapjack base.

My favourite dessert is a really wicked combination of pineapple- and coffee-soaked madeleines and chocolate marshmallow teacakes, all encased in a chocolate ganache – very indulgent but utterly yummy.

Other temptations that you will find in this chapter are a salty honey and apricot flan and a crispy summer berry cake – just the thing for warm sunshine dinners in the garden when summer fruits are in season.

Grown-up crispy cakes – deliciously naughty!

Store-bought meringues make a great store-cupboard ingredient.

Delicate meringue,
whipped cream and
fresh berries – a bowl
full of sunshine!

Blueberry compote, when
folded through cream,
gives such a vibrant hue.

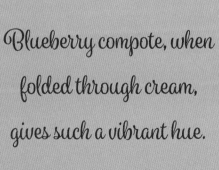

Traditional Eton Mess is made by stirring fruit and meringues through whipped cream to create a creamy fruit dessert. In this pretty version there is no stirring, so that the bowl has enticing layers. This is one of the easiest puddings I know to prepare, just slice the fruit, crush the meringue, whip the cream and "ta-dah" one scrumptious dessert – perfect for summer days!

Eton Mess Layer Dessert

SERVES 8
PREPARATION TIME 15 MINUTES, PLUS CHILLING

600ml/1 pint/2½ cups double (heavy) cream
5ml/1 tsp rose extract or rose syrup
30ml/2 tbsp icing (confectioners') sugar, sifted
100g/3½oz shop-brought meringue shells
400g/14oz/4 cups strawberries
300g/10oz/2½ cups raspberries

Equipment: electric mixer; a large glass serving bowl

1 Place the cream in a large mixing bowl with the rose extract and icing sugar and whisk to stiff peaks using an electric mixer. Taste for sweetness and add a little more icing sugar if you prefer a sweeter flavour.

2 Crush the meringue shells into small pieces using your hands.

3 Hull the strawberries and cut into thin slices.

4 Place a third of the cream over the base of the serving bowl and spread out in an even layer using a spatula. Sprinkle over half of the meringue pieces and half of the strawberry slices, distributing evenly.

5 Cover with a third of the cream and again spread out in an even layer. Sprinkle over the remaining meringue and top with the raspberries. Cover the fruit with the remaining cream mixture.

6 Chill in the refrigerator for at least an hour before serving. This dessert is best eaten on the day it is made.

For an autumnal version of this dessert try replacing the fruit with stewed plums and add a little ground cinnamon.

Everyone loves a crispy cake – and this is a grown-up version for adults to enjoy. It looks utterly kitsch but everyone who I have served this to just loves the combination of rich cream with the crunchy marshmallow crispy base and ripe berries. For the best flavour, use berries that are in season, and better yet pick them fresh from your garden or nearest obliging hedgerow.

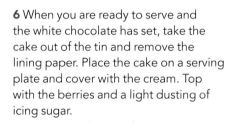

Crispy Fresh Berry Layer Cake

SERVES 8
PREPARATION TIME 20 MINUTES,
PLUS SETTING TIME

FOR THE BASE
225g/8oz/6 cups marshmallows
60g/2oz/½ stick butter
100g/3½oz/3½ cups rice crispies
100g/3½oz white chocolate

FOR THE TOPPING
225g/8oz clotted cream
400g/14oz/approx. 3 cups fresh berries
   of your choosing – I love to use
   strawberries, raspberries, blueberries
   and blackberries
Icing (confectioners') sugar, for dusting

Equipment: 23cm/9in round springform
tin or pan, greased and lined

1 Place the marshmallows and butter in a pan over a gentle heat until they have melted and are combined, stirring all the time.

2 Add the rice crispies to the pan and stir well so that all the crispies are coated in the marshmallow mixture.

3 Spoon the crispy mixture into the prepared tin and press down to an even layer with the back of a spoon.

4 Break the white chocolate into pieces and place in a heatproof bowl over a pan of simmering water. Simmer until the chocolate has melted, making sure that the base of the bowl does not touch the water.

5 Spread the melted chocolate over the top of the crispy cake layer and leave to set.

6 When you are ready to serve and the white chocolate has set, take the cake out of the tin and remove the lining paper. Place the cake on a serving plate and cover with the cream. Top with the berries and a light dusting of icing sugar.

7 As the cake contains fresh cream serve it straight away or store in the refrigerator. This cake should be eaten on the day it is made and will not keep.

For such an elegant dessert, a cake stand is a must when serving, whatever the occasion.

I made this cake to take to a talk I was giving for the South Bedfordshire Farmers Group. The gentlemen on the front row had thirds and declared it scrumptious and this was enough of a recommendation for this recipe to be included in the book. I love the combination of peanut butter and chocolate – the original sweet and salty pairing.

Peanut Chocolate Fudge Cake

SERVES 12
PREPARATION TIME 30 MINUTES, PLUS CHILLING

FOR THE BASE
400g/14oz chocolate brownies

FOR THE PEANUT MOUSSE
360g/12¾oz/1½ cups cream cheese
250g/9oz crunchy peanut butter
30ml/2 tbsp caster (superfine) sugar
250ml/8fl oz/1 cup double (heavy) cream

FOR THE TOPPING
60g/2oz white chocolate
45ml/3 tbsp finely chopped salted peanuts, finely chopped
12 Reece's mini peanut butter cups

Equipment: 23cm/9in round loose-bottomed tart tin or pie pan, greased and lined

1 Press the brownies into the base of the tin, squashing down with the back of a spoon or with clean fingers to ensure that there are no gaps in the base.

2 For the peanut mousse, place the cream cheese, peanut butter and sugar in a mixing bowl and whisk together for a few minutes. Add the cream to the bowl and scrape the mixture away from the sides of the bowl. Whisk together until the cream thickens and the mixture is stiff, then spoon into the prepared tin on top of the brownies and chill in the refrigerator.

3 Place the white chocolate in a heatproof bowl over a pan of simmering water and heat until the chocolate has melted, stirring occasionally. It is important that the bottom of the bowl does not touch the water in the pan. Allow the chocolate to cool for about 10 minutes.

4 Remove the cake tin from the refrigerator and drizzle big circles of the cooled chocolate over the top of the peanut mousse using a spoon. Sprinkle over the chopped peanuts and decorate with the mini peanut butter cups.

5 Chill in the refrigerator for at least 3 hours before serving. This dessert will store in the refrigerator for up to 3 days.

If you cannot find Reece's mini peanut butter cups, decorate with other peanut candies, such as M&M's or chopped honey-roasted peanuts.

This cake has such a pretty delicate purple and white colour that it looks simply spectacular as the centrepiece of a dessert table. Made with readymade flapjacks and topped with fresh blueberry compote and white chocolate curls it is an easy dessert to assemble in advance of a supper party or lunch gathering.

White Chocolate and Blueberry Layer Cake

SERVES 12
PREPARATION TIME 30 MINUTES, PLUS CHILLING

FOR THE BLUEBERRY COMPOTE AND SYRUP
50g/1¾oz/¼ cup caster (superfine) sugar
250g/9oz/1 cup blueberries
Juice of 2 lemons

FOR THE BASE AND TOPPING
300g/10⅔oz soft flapjacks
120g/4oz white chocolate
150ml/¼ pint/⅔ cup crème fraîche
250g/9oz mascarpone cheese

Equipment: 23cm/9in round loose-bottomed cake tin or pan, greased and lined; swivel vegetable peeler

1 Place the sugar, blueberries and lemon juice in a pan and simmer over a gentle heat for about 5 minutes until the fruit is very soft and the liquid is syrupy. Place a fine mesh sieve or strainer over a bowl and pour in the cooked blueberries to separate the fruit and the syrup. Do not press the fruit down as you want the fruit to remain juicy. Leave to cool.

2 Press the flapjacks into the base of the tin, pressing them down with your hands so that they form a complete layer.

3 Using a swivel peeler, make chocolate curls with around 20g/¾oz of the white chocolate by pulling the peeler along the long edge of the chocolate bar. It is important that the chocolate is at room temperature to make the best curls.

4 Place the remaining white chocolate in a heatproof bowl resting over a pan of simmering water and simmer until the chocolate has melted. Spoon the melted white chocolate over the flapjack base and spread out, then spread over the blueberry fruit.

5 In a separate bowl, whisk together most of the blueberry syrup, crème fraîche and mascarpone cheese until the mixture is thick. Spoon into the tin on top of the fruit and spread out into an even layer.

6 Drizzle over the remaining blueberry syrup and swirl in, using a fork to make a decorative pattern. Top the dessert with the white chocolate curls and chill in the refrigerator for 3 hours.

One summer I went to Switzerland with my friend Maren where fresh apricots were sold at almost every roadside, filling the air with a honey perfume. Apricots are often an overlooked fruit. If like me your early associations of this fruit are the rather plain apricot jam, then let me help dispel this gross injustice. Ripe apricots are completely different and add a lovely fruity dimension to this dessert.

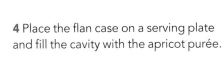

Salted Honey and Apricot Flan

SERVES 8
PREPARATION TIME 30 MINUTES

16 ripe apricots
30ml/2 tbsp clear honey
30ml/2 tbsp caster (superfine) sugar
Juice of 2 lemons
300ml/½ pint/¼ cup double (heavy) cream
180g/6¼oz/¾ cup cream cheese
Pinch of salt
1 large flan case (approximately 25cm/10in)
30ml/2 tbsp apricot glaze or jam
30ml/2 tbsp pistachio nuts, finely chopped

Equipment: food processor or blender; piping or pastry bag fitted with a large star nozzle; serving plate; pastry brush

1 To prepare the apricots, place them in a pan and cover with water, add 15ml/1 tbsp of honey and simmer for about 5–8 minutes until the fruit is soft. Remove from the heat and drain the water. When cool enough to handle, cut a slit into the skin of each apricot and remove the skins. Cut the peeled apricots in half and remove the stones or pits.

2 Reserve half of the apricots and blitz the remainder in a blender with 30ml/2 tbsp of sugar and the juice of one of the lemons to a smooth purée.

3 In a mixing bowl, whisk together the cream, cream cheese, the remaining honey and salt until smooth and thick. Spoon into a piping bag.

4 Place the flan case on a serving plate and fill the cavity with the apricot purée.

5 Pipe the cream in a circle of stars around the edge of the flan case. Place the apricot halves inside the circle of cream stars.

6 Heat the apricot glaze and remaining lemon juice in a pan until the glaze has dissolved. Allow to cool for a few minutes, then using a pastry brush, brush the glaze over the apricots. You may not need all of the glaze.

7 Sprinkle the top of the cream stars with the chopped pistachio nuts and serve immediately with pouring cream if you wish. This flan will not keep and should be served as soon as you have assembled it.

Shop-bought flan cases come in various sizes so if you cannot find a large one, make two smaller ones instead.

The inspiration for this dessert came from a holiday to Bali where a wonderful chef called Penny taught cooking classes in a hut in a rice paddy field! It was a magical experience. In her restaurant at our hotel she served a dessert of whipped cream chocolate brownies and rum-soaked raisins – so delicious we ate it nearly every evening. Using ready-made brownies means this dessert requires minimal effort and yet the result is a rich and indulgent rum truffle cake.

Rum and Raisin Brownie Torte

1 Place the rum in a pan and heat until just warm then tip in the raisins; do not boil, remove from the heat and leave to cool. The raisins should become plump from the liquid.

2 Place the eggs, cream and milk in a large jug or pitcher and whisk together, then pour into a pan. Break up 300g/11oz of the chocolate into small pieces and place in a pan with the cream mixture. Heat over a gentle heat, whisking all the time, for about 4–5 minutes until the chocolate is melted and the ganache is thick and glossy.

3 Stir in the rum-soaked raisins and golden syrup and set aside whilst you prepare the base.

4 Break the brownies into small pieces and spread out over the base of the tin. It does not matter if there are small gaps. If the seal of your tin is not tight, wrap the base and sides of the tin in foil to ensure that the ganache does not leak out of the tin.

5 Pour the rum and raisin ganache over the brownies and chill in the refrigerator overnight to set.

6 When you are ready to serve, remove the cake from the tin by sliding a sharp knife around the edge of the tin and remove the sides. Place the cake on a serving plate and decorate by grating over the remaining chocolate. Serve with a dollop of whipped cream. This cake will store for up to 3 days in the refrigerator.

SERVES 16
PREPARATION TIME 30 MINUTES, PLUS CHILLING

FOR THE GANACHE TOPPING
125ml/4fl oz/½ cup dark rum
150g/5oz/1 cup raisins
2 eggs
375ml/13fl oz/1½ cups double (heavy) cream, plus extra whipped to serve
125ml/4fl oz/½ cup milk
350g/12½oz plain (semisweet) chocolate, minimum 70% cocoa solids
15ml/1 tbsp golden (light corn) syrup

FOR THE BASE
150g/5⅓oz chocolate brownies

Equipment: 23cm/9in loose-bottomed deep cake tin or pan, greased and lined; foil; grater

If you don't like rum you can substitute a coffee liqueur, such as Tia Maria or Amaretto.

This truffle cake may sound an unusual combination but you are going to have to trust me that pineapple, coffee and chocolate go well together. This cake contains one of my favourite naughty treats – marshmallow teacakes! They hold their domed shape in the dessert and so make an attractive contrast of white marshmallow nestling in the dark truffle ganache. Fresh pineapple has more flavour than tinned so use this if you are able to.

Pineapple and Coffee Truffle Cake

SERVES 12
PREPARATION TIME 30 MINUTES, PLUS CHILLING

FOR THE BASE
300g/10oz Oreo or similar chocolate cookies
125g/4½oz/9 tbsp butter

FOR THE FILLING
6 chocolate marshmallow teacakes
5 or 6 large madeleines or vanilla
   sponge cakes
15ml/1 tbsp instant coffee granules
125ml/4fl oz/½ cup coffee liqueur
   (such as Kalhua)
200g/7oz/approx. 1 cup fresh or tinned/
   canned pineapple (drained weight)

FOR THE GANACHE TOPPING
200g/7oz plain (semisweet) chocolate,
   ideally 85% cocoa solids
250ml/8fl oz/1 cup double (heavy) cream
80ml/2½fl oz/⅓ cup coffee liqueur
   (such as Kalhua)
1 egg
Chocolate curls, to decorate

Equipment: food processor or blender;
   23cm/9in round springform cake tin
   or pan, greased and lined; swivel
   vegetable peeler

1 Begin by preparing the base of the cake. Crush the Oreo cookies to fine crumbs in a food processor or blender. Melt the butter in a pan over the heat, cool slightly and then stir into the biscuit crumbs so that they are all coated.

2 Press the crumbs into the base of the tin with the back of a spoon in an even layer.

3 Unwrap the teacakes and place 5 in a ring around the edge of the tin with gaps in between, and place the remaining teacake in the centre of the tin.

4 Dissolve the instant coffee granules in 80ml/2½fl oz/⅓ cup of boiling water and leave to cool. Add the coffee liqueur and one by one soak the madeleines or cakes in the mixture. You want them to absorb the liquid but not become too soggy. It is best to do this one by one so that you can ensure the right consistency.

5 Place the soaked cakes over the biscuit base in the gaps between the teacakes so that the whole base is covered in a layer of cakes.

6 Evenly distribute the pineapple on top of the soaked cakes.

7 For the ganache layer, break the chocolate into small pieces. In a jug or pitcher whisk together the cream, liqueur and the egg, until the egg is blended with the cream. Pour the cream mixture into a pan with the chocolate pieces and heat over a gentle heat until the chocolate has melted and the ganache is smooth, whisking all the time.

8 Leave the ganache to cool slightly (so that it doesn't melt the teacakes) and then pour over the base of the cake and spread out in an even layer. Sprinkle with chocolate curls to decorate. Make these by running a swivel vegetable peeler along the long edge of a bar of chocolate. It is important that the chocolate is at room temperature and not chilled for the best result.

9 Chill the cake in the refrigerator for at least 3 hours then cut into slices to serve. This cake will keep for up to 3 days in the refrigerator.

The humble pretzel is such an under-utilized ingredient in desserts. I love the salty taste dimension it can add to cakes and puddings. This recipe is a perfect example. If you do not have time to make cinnamon syrup, you can buy it from good coffee shops or online. This cake is made in an inverted form and you turn the cake out to reveal the pretty pretzel decoration just before serving.

Cinnamon Pretzel Crunchie Cake

SPECTACULAR CAKES AND CENTREPIECE DESSERTS

SERVES 12
PREPARATION TIME 30 MINUTES, PLUS CHILLING

FOR THE CINNAMON SYRUP
50g/1¾oz/¼ cup caster (superfine) sugar
10ml/2 tsp ground cinnamon

FOR THE CHEESECAKE LAYER
360g/12¾oz/1½ cups cream cheese
250ml/8fl oz/1 cup double (heavy) cream

FOR THE PRETZEL CRUNCH LAYER
150g/5oz salted pretzels
100g/3½oz/7tbsp butter
30ml/2 tbsp caster (superfine) sugar

FOR THE CHOCOLATE MOUSSE
180g/6½oz plain (semisweet) chocolate
5ml/1 tsp ground cinnamon
2 eggs
50g/1¾oz/¼ cup caster (superfine) sugar
250ml/8fl oz/1 cup double (heavy) cream

FOR THE BISCUIT LAYER
150g/5oz Oreo or similar chocolate cookies
60g/2oz/4 tbsp butter

Equipment: food processor or blender; 23cm/9in round springform tin or pan, greased and lined with a double layer of clear film or plastic wrap on the base so that you can turn the cake out; mixer

1 Begin by preparing the cinnamon syrup. Simmer 40ml/8 tsp of water, the sugar and ground cinnamon in a small pan until you have a sticky syrup. This will take about 5 minutes. Leave to cool then pour into a large mixing bowl and whisk with the cream cheese until smooth. Add the double cream and whisk slowly until the mixture starts to thicken.

2 Place sufficient whole pretzels to cover the prepared tin in a pretty pattern. Spoon the cinnamon cheesecake carefully over the pretzels, smoothing down gently using a spatula but taking care that you do not move the pretzels so that they retain their decorative pattern.

3 Blitz the remaining pretzels in a food processor or blender to fine crumbs. Melt the butter and sugar in a pan and stir in the pretzel crumbs, mixing in so that all of the crumbs are coated. Spoon the pretzel mixture over the cinnamon cheesecake and press down level with the back of a spoon. Chill in the refrigerator whilst you make the chocolate mousse.

4 For the chocolate mousse, break the chocolate into small pieces and place in a heatproof bowl resting over a pan of simmering water and simmer until the chocolate has melted. Add the cinnamon syrup to the chocolate, whisk in and leave to cool slightly. Separate the eggs and place the yolks and caster sugar in one mixing bowl and the whites in another.

5 Whisk the yolks and sugar with a mixer until they are very pale yellow and thick. Add the slightly cooled cinnamon chocolate to the mixture and whisk in. Add the cream and whisk again until the mixture thickens.

6 Whisk the egg whites with clean dry beaters until they hold stiff peaks when you lift the beaters, and then fold into the chocolate mixture. You should fold in gently so that as much air is retained in the mousse as possible. Spoon the chocolate cinnamon mousse over the pretzel layer.

7 Crush the Oreos to fine crumbs in a food processor. Melt the butter in a pan over the heat then stir into the crumbs. Spread the crumbs over the cinnamon chocolate mousse in a flat layer. Chill in the refrigerator overnight.

8 To serve, slide a knife around the edge of the tin and remove the sides. Place a serving plate on top of the cake and then holding the base of the tin and plate tightly, invert the cake so that the base of the tin is on top of the cake. Carefully remove the tin base and the clear film. The cake will store for up to 3 days in the refrigerator.

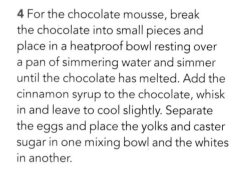

Ice Cream Cakes

When days are hot and sunny, everyone loves to eat ice cream – I know I do! This chapter therefore contains a selection of wonderful ice cream desserts to serve when the sun is shining.

Ice cream bombes are quick to prepare and look stunning when you cut into them. This chapter contains two delectable versions – a sour cherry one nestled in swirls of Swiss roll that looks very elegant when you cut into it and a coconut, honey and dark chocolate bombe, made with homemade ice cream and topped with toasted coconut.

For children's parties in place of a birthday cake why not serve the chocolate wafer ice cream cake or the bright and colourful jelly and ice cream layer cake. Kids will love these delicious ice cream treats.

For more simple occasions, there are Neapolitan cookie crumb pots and a scrumptious peanut butter ice cream pie, or for a hot and cold dessert you can try the toffee apple ice cream pie served with a hot sauce which melts the ice cream. Grab your spoons and dig in!

With multiple pink, yellow and chocolate stripes, these ice cream desserts are as pretty as a picture.

Warm caramel sauce poured over apple ice cream pie will make everyone smile.

Ice cream cakes store well
in the freezer so make a
perfect stand-by dessert.

It is amazing the decorative patterns you can achieve in this dessert with a humble Swiss roll (or jelly roll as it is known in America). When you cut slices of this bomb the outer layer has pretty stripes encasing the ice cream and frozen cherries. I love to serve this dessert with a warm chocolate sauce on the side to pour over the top. It melts the ice cream and frozen cherry compote a little, making this one wickedly indulgent cake.

Sour Cherry Ice Cream Bombe

SERVES 8–10
PREPARATION TIME 15 MINUTES,
PLUS OVERNIGHT FREEZING

FOR THE BOMBE
1 Swiss or jelly roll
500ml/17fl oz/2 cups cookies and cream ice cream or chocolate chip ice cream
50g/1¾oz/½ cup dried sour cherries
250ml/8fl oz/1 cup chocolate ice cream
250ml/8fl oz/1 cup cherry compote

FOR THE CHOCOLATE SAUCE
250ml/8fl oz/1 cup double (heavy) cream
125ml/4fl oz/½ cup milk
100g/3½oz plain (semisweet) chocolate, broken into pieces
50g/1¾oz/7 tbsp butter
15ml/1 tbsp golden (light corn) syrup
15ml/1 tbsp Kirsch (optional)

Equipment: one large pudding basin or freezerproof bowl, lined with clear film or plastic wrap

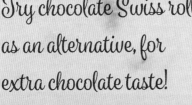

Try chocolate Swiss roll as an alternative, for extra chocolate taste!

1 Line the pudding basin with clear film following the instructions on page 19. Cut the Swiss roll into slices and use them to line the inside of the basin in an even layer. When you reach the top of the basin, if necessary, cut the Swiss roll into half slices to fill in the gaps so that the Swiss roll covers the edge of the bowl completely.

2 Bring all the ice cream to room temperature until it is just soft enough to spoon out. Place spoonfuls of the cookies and cream or chocolate chip ice cream into the Swiss roll-lined basin and spread out into an even thick layer, covering all of the Swiss roll but leaving a vacant dome-shaped area in the centre of the basin for the other layers.

3 Press the dried sour cherries into the ice cream in the basin and then cover with a layer of the chocolate ice cream, leaving a cavity in the centre. Fill the centre of the bombe with the cherry compote until it is full. You may not need all of the compote. Cover the top of the bombe with a layer of clear film and freeze until solid.

4 When you are ready to serve place the cream, milk, chocolate, butter and syrup in a pan and heat until the butter and chocolate have melted. Whisk until you have a smooth sauce adding the Kirsch, if you are using, for a nice boozy kick.

5 Remove the ice cream bombe from the freezer and invert on to a plate. Remove the basin and clear film and leave for a few minutes until the ice cream becomes soft enough to cut into slices. Pour the warm sauce over the slices of ice cream bombe and serve.

The Italian pink, yellow and chocolate ice cream Neapolitan is a kitsch classic, loved by kids and adults alike. These little ice cream pots are quick to prepare and can be kept in the freezer until you are ready to serve. With crumbly cheesecake layers and multiple pink, yellow and chocolate ice cream stripes, these cakes are as pretty as a picture.

Neapolitan Cookie Crumb Towers

SERVES 6
**PREPARATION TIME 20 MINUTES,
PLUS FREEZING**

85g/3oz pink wafer biscuits or cookies
100g/3½oz digestive biscuits or graham crackers
100g/3½oz Oreo or similar chocolate cookies
125g/4½oz/9 tbsp butter
About 1 litre/1¾ pints/4 cups Neapolitan ice cream

Equipment: food processor or blender; 6 tall serving pots or glasses

You can make this recipe in chef's rings as an alternative to glasses.

1 In the food processor or blender, first blitz the pink wafer biscuits to fine crumbs then tip into a bowl. Next blitz the digestive biscuits to fine crumbs and tip into a second bowl. Finally blitz the Oreo cookies to fine crumbs and place in a third bowl. It is important to blitz in this light to dark order so that the colour of the cookies are clearly defined.

2 Melt the butter in a pan and stir a third of the butter into each of the crumb mixtures. Leave to cool.

3 Add layers of the ice cream into each serving pot or glass in any order you choose so that you have one layer of each flavour in each pot, sandwiched with all three biscuit layer stripes.

4 Working quickly, cover each chocolate ice cream layer with a layer of the chocolate crumb biscuit mixture, pressing down with a spoon. Cover each strawberry layer with pink wafer biscuit crumbs and cover each vanilla layer with digestive biscuit crumbs, so that you have stripy layers. The top layer on each ice cream stack should be a biscuit crumb layer of the same colour of the ice cream below.

5 Return to the freezer to set. It is best to assemble one pot or glass at a time and then place in the freezer straight away.

6 Remove from the freezer and bring to room temperature for a few minutes before serving.

This cake takes the perfect two ingredients for any children's party and transforms them into a spectacular stripy dessert. For a more indulgent version you can replace the jelly layers with pretty coloured sorbets – such as orange and raspberry – which will give a stronger flavour. But the jelly layers once frozen are "sorbet-like" and more economical. If you want you can put fruit in the jelly layer to add additional flavour – such as mandarin segments in the orange jelly.

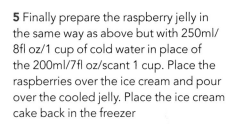

Jelly and Ice Cream Cake

SERVES 10
PREPARATION TIME 30 MINUTES, PLUS 2–3 DAYS FREEZING

1 x 135g/4½oz packet of orange jelly cubes
Juice of 1 large orange
2 litres/3½ pints/8 cups vanilla ice cream
1 x 135g/4½oz packet of lime jelly cubes
Juice of 2 limes
1 x 135g/4½oz packet of raspberry jelly cubes
200g/7oz/generous 1½ cups fresh raspberries

Equipment: 23cm/9in round loose-bottomed cake tin or pan; clear film or plastic wrap

1 Begin by preparing the cake tin. You need to make sure that the tin does not leak so unless your tin has a very tight fitting seal, wrap the base and sides of the tin in a good few layers of clear film to ensure that the jelly does not escape when you pour it in. You can test if your tin is watertight by adding water to it and seeing if it leaks.

2 Dissolve the orange jelly in 250ml/8fl oz/1 cup of boiling water and leave to cool, stirring to ensure that the jelly melts. Add the orange juice to the jelly and a further 200ml/7fl oz/scant 1 cup of cold water then pour into the tin and transfer to the freezer to set. The jelly needs to be completely frozen solid before you add the next layer. The length of time for this to happen will depend on the temperature of your freezer but it should be about 4 or 5 hours.

3 When the jelly has frozen, bring the ice cream to room temperature until it is just soft enough to scoop. Remove the tin from the freezer and cover the jelly with a third of the ice cream, smoothing it down so that it makes a flat layer covering the jelly completely. Return to the freezer until the ice cream is frozen solid.

4 Next prepare the lime jelly in the same way as the orange jelly, adding the lime juice in place of the orange juice. Repeat the freezing and ice cream layers as above. It is important that the jelly is completely cold before you pour it over otherwise it will melt the ice cream layer below.

5 Finally prepare the raspberry jelly in the same way as above but with 250ml/8fl oz/1 cup of cold water in place of the 200ml/7fl oz/scant 1 cup. Place the raspberries over the ice cream and pour over the cooled jelly. Place the ice cream cake back in the freezer

6 When ready to serve, remove the ice cream cake from the freezer and leave to come to room temperature for about 15 minutes. Remove the clear film and carefully slide a sharp knife around the edge of the tin and remove the sides the tin. Remove the base and place the dessert on a large plate or cake stand. Use a warm knife, held under the hot tap, to cut the cake. The cake will store in the freezer for up to 1 month.

This cake does take a few days to prepare but it certainly has the "wow" factor when you bring it out to serve!

This is a delicious ice cream cake bursting with peanuts and caramel sauce. It is made in a loaf tin with a thick peanut biscuit case so looks very special when you serve it cut into wedges, with the caramel ribbon running through, topped with peanut cream and chopped peanuts. It is important to use smooth peanut butter in the topping otherwise the peanuts can get stuck in the icing nozzle.

Peanut Butter Ice Cream Cake

SERVES 10
PREPARATION TIME 30 MINUTES, PLUS FREEZING

FOR THE BISCUIT CASE
300g/10oz peanut cookies
125g/4½oz/9 tbsp butter

FOR THE FILLING
45ml/3 tbsp salted peanuts
60ml/4 tbsp salted caramel sauce or thick
  toffee sauce (available in supermarkets),
  or follow the recipe on p101 adding salt
500ml/17fl oz/2 cups peanut butter
  ice cream

FOR THE PEANUT CREAM TOPPING
30ml/2 tbsp smooth peanut butter
250ml/8fl oz/1 cup double (heavy) cream
15ml/1 tbsp icing (confectioners')
  sugar, sifted
15ml/1 tbsp salted peanuts, finely chopped

Equipment: food processor or blender;
  1 loaf tin or pan, greased and lined with
  baking parchment; mixer; piping or
  pastry bag, fitted with a large star nozzle

1 Crush the peanut cookies to fine crumbs in a food processor. Melt the butter in a pan, leave to cool slightly and then stir into the crumbs so that they are all coated in butter.

If you can't find peanut butter ice cream substitute vanilla or chocolate instead.

2 Press the crumbs into the base and sides of the loaf tin in a thick layer. If the crumbs are too crumbly add a little more melted butter. You need the crumbs to hold their shape up the sides of the tin so that you have a case to put the ice cream in.

3 Place the tin in the freezer to chill. It is important that the baking parchment hangs over the edges of the tin as this is needed to help you lift the ice cream pie out of the tin when you are ready to serve, so do not scrimp on the baking parchment.

4 Stir the peanuts into the caramel sauce and set aside. Bring the ice cream to room temperature so that it is just soft enough to spoon out.

5 Remove the loaf tin from the freezer and place half of the ice cream into the base of the biscuit case, spreading it out into an even layer.

6 Spoon the peanut and caramel mixture on the ice cream in an even layer to cover over.

7 Cover with the remaining ice cream in an even layer and return to the freezer.

8 When you are ready to serve place the peanut butter, cream and icing sugar in a mixing bowl and using a mixer, whisk until the cream holds a stiff peak. Spoon the mixture into the piping bag and pipe into stars over the top of the ice cream pie. Sprinkle with the finely chopped peanuts.

9 Serve immediately. Any uneaten pie can be returned to the freezer and stored for up to a month, provided that the ice cream is still frozen when you return it to the freezer. You should not refreeze melted ice cream.

This is a great dessert that you can prepare ahead and keep in the freezer, just making the streusel topping and blueberry compote a little while before you want to serve. The dessert uses readymade flapjacks although you can make your own if you do want to bake.

Blueberry Streusel Ice Cream Cake

SERVES 8
PREPARATION TIME 30 MINUTES,
PLUS FREEZING

FOR THE CASE AND FILLING
350g/12½oz flapjacks
500ml/17fl oz/2 cups vanilla ice cream

FOR THE BLUEBERRY COMPOTE
250g/9oz/1 cup blueberries
60g/2oz/½ cup caster (superfine) sugar
Juice of 2 limes

FOR THE STREUSEL TOPPING
45g/1½oz amaretti
60g/2oz flapjacks
50g/1¾oz golden or white marzipan
45g/1½oz/3 tbsp butter

*Equipment: 20cm/8in round x 4cm/1½in
deep pie dish, greased and lined*

1 Press the flapjacks for the case into the prepared pie dish with your fingers, ensuring that there are no gaps and the flapjack is in an even layer over the base and sides of your dish. You need to ensure that the flapjacks you use are soft so that they can be easily pressed into shape.

2 Place the flapjack base in the freezer for 10 minutes to chill it – this will help prevent the ice cream from melting. Bring the vanilla ice cream to room temperature so that it is just soft enough to spoon out. Fill the flapjack case with the ice cream and smooth level. Return to the freezer until you are ready to serve.

3 For the compote, place the blueberries, sugar and lime juice in a pan and simmer for about 5 minutes until the fruit has burst and the sauce is thick. Set aside to cool completely.

4 For the topping, crush the amaretti into small pieces with your hands in a bowl. Add the flapjacks to your mixture and mix together with your hands. Break the marzipan into small pieces and add to the bowl. Melt the butter in a pan and whilst it is still hot pour over the topping mixture. Mix together with your hands so that the streusel forms small clumps.

5 To serve, remove the pie from the freezer and top with the compote and streusel topping. Serve straight away.

This is a delicious and elegant ice cream dessert made with homemade ice cream. I love the combination of honey, coconut and bitter chocolate and this bombe looks quite dramatic with its black, white and yellow layers. Different honeys can vary in sweetness so taste the honey ice cream before churning and add a little more honey if you wish.

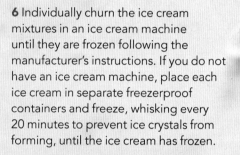

Coconut Honey Ice Cream Bombe

SERVES 10
PREPARATION TIME 40 MINUTES,
PLUS FREEZING

FOR THE COCONUT ICE CREAM
80g/3oz/½ cup caster (superfine) sugar
3 egg yolks
400ml/14fl oz/1½ cups coconut milk
200ml/7fl oz/1 cup double (heavy) cream

FOR THE HONEY ICE CREAM
2 egg yolks
30ml/2 tbsp honey
300ml/½ pint/1¼ cups milk
100ml/3½fl oz/½ cup double (heavy) cream
Yellow food colouring (optional)

TO ASSEMBLE
60ml/4 tbsp coconut shavings
100g/3½oz dark (bittersweet) chocolate chunks
100g/3½oz plain (semisweet) chocolate

Equipment: ice cream machine (optional);
1 large pudding basin or freezerproof
bowl; clear film or plastic wrap

1 First toast the coconut shavings for the decoration in a dry frying pan until golden brown. Stir all the time as it can burn easily. Remove from the heat and tip into a bowl. Once cool, store in an airtight container until needed.

2 For the coconut ice cream, whisk together the sugar and egg yolks until they have doubled in size and are very thick and creamy.

3 Heat the coconut milk and cream in a pan and bring to the boil. Whilst whisking the egg mixture, pour over the hot coconut milk in a steady stream. Whisk until the mixture is smooth. Return the pan to the heat and whisk for a few minutes until the mixture starts to thicken. Remove from the heat and leave to cool.

4 Next prepare the honey ice cream mixture. Whisk the egg yolks and honey together in a mixing bowl until the mixture is thick and creamy and has doubled in size. Heat the milk and cream in a pan and bring to the boil. Pour the boiling milk over the egg mixture, whisking all the time.

5 Return the pan to the heat and heat for a few minutes until the mixture starts to thicken adding a little yellow food colouring, if using. Leave to cool completely.

6 Individually churn the ice cream mixtures in an ice cream machine until they are frozen following the manufacturer's instructions. If you do not have an ice cream machine, place each ice cream in separate freezerproof containers and freeze, whisking every 20 minutes to prevent ice crystals from forming, until the ice cream has frozen.

7 Line the pudding basin with a double layer of clear film following the instructions on page 19. Begin assembling the bombe by filling it with a thick layer of the coconut ice cream, leaving a dome-shaped cavity in the centre. Sprinkle over the dark chocolate chunks so that they cover the whole inside of the cavity of the coconut ice cream. You need to work quickly so that the ice cream does not melt.

8 Fill the cavity with the honey ice cream. You may not need it all depending on the size of your basin so store any extra in a separate container in the freezer. Place the bombe in the freezer overnight.

9 When you are ready to serve place the plain chocolate in a heatproof bowl resting over a pan of simmering water and simmer until melted then leave to cool. Remove the bombe from the freezer and bring to room temperature for a few minutes. Invert on to a serving plate and remove the bowl and clear film.

10 Drizzle over the cooled chocolate in a pretty pattern and decorate with the toasted coconut. Serve straight away.

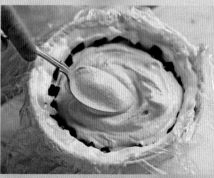

I have several apple trees in my garden and in the autumn harvest I love to use them for desserts. The warm toffee sauce, apple compote and ice cream are a match made in heaven. As an alternative you can fill the biscuit case with the apple compote and ice cream so the apple compote will form a firm sorbet. I like it both ways.

Toffee Apple Ice Cream Pie

SERVES 10
PREPARATION TIME 30 MINUTES, PLUS FREEZING

FOR THE APPLE COMPOTE
900g/2lb cooking apples (approximately 3 large apples)
Juice of 1 lemon
100g/3½oz/½ cup caster (superfine) sugar

FOR THE BISCUIT CASE AND ICE CREAM FILLING
300g/10oz caramel biscuits or cookies, such as Lotus
125g/4oz/9 tbsp butter
1 litre/1¾ pints/4 cups vanilla ice cream

FOR THE TOFFEE SAUCE
60g/2oz/¼ cup light brown sugar
50g/1¾oz/3½ tbsp butter
125/4fl oz/½ cup double (heavy) cream
80ml/2½fl oz/⅓ cup milk

Equipment: food processor or blender; 23cm/9in round loose-bottomed cake tin or pan, greased and lined

1 Peel and core the apples and chop into small pieces approximately 2.5cm/1in in size and place in a pan with the lemon juice, sugar and about 150ml/¼ pint/⅔ cup of water. Simmer for about 10 minutes until apple is soft. If the apples become too dry add a little more water to the pan. Once the apple is soft, leave to cool.

2 Crush the biscuits to fine crumbs in a food processor. Melt the butter in a pan and then stir into the biscuit crumbs so that all the crumbs are coated in butter. Press the crumbs into the base and sides of the tin, coming about 5cm/2in up the sides of the tin. Chill in the refrigerator.

3 Bring the ice cream to room temperature so that it is just soft enough to spoon out, and fill the biscuit case with the ice cream. Return to the freezer to set firm.

4 To prepare the toffee sauce, heat the light brown sugar and butter in a pan until melted and caramelized, taking care that the mixture does not burn. Add the cream and milk to the pan and stir until you have a thick caramel sauce. Do not worry if the sugar crystallizes into lumps when you add the liquid, as these will dissolve as you heat the mixture.

5 When you are ready to serve, remove the ice cream pie from the freezer and bring to room temperature so that the ice cream is just soft enough to cut into slices.

6 Remove from the tin and place on a serving plate and top with the apple compote. Serve portions of the ice cream pie with the warm toffee sauce which will melt the ice cream a little – delicious!

If you cannot find caramel biscuits use digestives or graham crackers instead.

This cake is a perfect party centrepiece for those who do not have much time. You can prepare the ice cream centre in advance and then just assemble the cake shortly before serving. As the cake contains ice cream you need to serve it quickly before it starts to melt. You can top with any sweets you like – chocolate candies work well but multi-coloured jelly beans would also look fun!

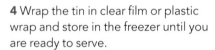

KitKat Ice Cream Cake

SERVES 10
PREPARATION TIME 30 MINUTES, PLUS FREEZING

150g/5oz Oreo or similar chocolate cookies
80g/3oz/5½ tbsp butter
1 litre/1¾ pints/4 cups vanilla ice cream
7–8 four-finger KitKats or similar chocolate wafer fingers
300g/10oz/2 cups white and brown chocolate-coated candies, such as Smarties or M&Ms

Equipment: food processor or blender; 20cm/8in loose-bottomed deep round cake tin or pan, lined; decorative ribbon

1 Place the Oreo cookies in a food processor or blender and blitz to fine crumbs. Melt the butter in a pan and then stir into the cookie crumbs, stirring well so that all the crumbs are coated. Leave until cool.

2 Remove the ice cream from the freezer and leave for a few minutes until just soft enough to handle.

3 Spread half of the cookie crumbs over the base of the tin and press down to compact with the back of a spoon. Spoon over half of the ice cream and press down. Cover with the remaining biscuit crumbs and press down using the back of a spoon. Cover with the remaining ice cream, smoothing down as before.

4 Wrap the tin in clear film or plastic wrap and store in the freezer until you are ready to serve.

5 To serve, remove the clear film from the tin and slide a knife around the edge of the cake and remove from the tin. Place on a serving plate.

6 Break the chocolate wafers into individual sticks and place around the edge of the cake so that they are touching. Tie a ribbon around the cake to hold the wafer sticks in place. It is best to have someone to help you with the assembly. Cover the top of the cake with the chocolate candies and serve immediately.

The chocolate wafer sticks and chocolate candies make this dessert a chocoholic's delight!

No-Bake Cheesecakes

I love to make cheesecake – it is one of those desserts that everyone enjoys no matter how old or young they are. Rather than classic baked cheesecakes, this chapter contains the lighter, but no less delicious, refrigerator cheesecakes that are ready to serve after chilling for around 3 hours.

All of your favourite flavours are included here – strawberry and chocolate, topped with fresh berries and set with strawberry jelly; banana and walnut; and a rich and indulgent white chocolate pistachio cheesecake.

For citrus lovers there is a St. Clements cheesecake, bursting with a fruity tang; or a zesty and rich lemon caramel cheesecake, topped with caramel swirls.

Anyone with a sweet tooth will love the candy cheesecakes such as the almond brittle cheesecake or the malted cheesecake pie, topped with chocolate malt balls. Why not make them all and host a cheesecake party?

The sharpness of the lemon cuts through the buttery caramel, making this one of my all-time favourites.

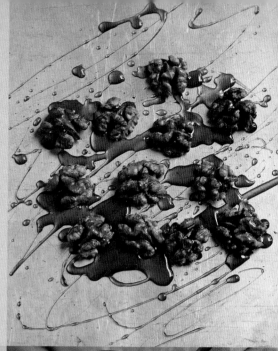

A delicious malted biscuit base is filled with malted cream and topped with a rich chocolate ganache.

One of those perfect combinations – rich and indulgent with a burst of sunshine fruit.

This zesty tangy cheesecake makes a light dinner party dessert.

Strawberries and chocolate are one of those perfect combinations – rich and indulgent with a burst of sunshine fruit. I love to serve this cheesecake after picking ripe berries at my local fruit farm. If you want to simplify the recipe you can omit the chocolate ganache topping and just pile the cheesecake high with fresh berries and curls of dark chocolate instead, for an equally spectacular dessert.

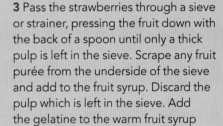

Strawberry Jelly Cheesecake

SERVES 12
PREPARATION TIME 30 MINUTES,
PLUS CHILLING

FOR THE BASE
300g/10oz digestive biscuits (graham crackers)
30ml/2 tbsp cocoa powder, sifted
100g/3½oz/7 tbsp butter

FOR THE CHEESECAKE
600g/1lb 4oz/3½ cups ripe strawberries
100g/3½oz/½ cup caster (superfine) sugar
15ml/1 tbsp powdered gelatine
135g/4½oz packet of strawberry jelly cubes
300g/10oz/1¼ cups cream cheese
150ml/¼ pint/⅔ cup double (heavy) cream

FOR THE GANACHE TOPPING
150g/5oz plain (semisweet) chocolate
80ml/2½fl oz/⅓ cup double (heavy) cream
15ml/1 tbsp butter

Equipment: food processor or blender; 25cm/10in loose-bottomed round cake tin or pan, greased and lined

1 For the base, crush the digestive biscuits to fine crumbs in a food processor or blender or place the biscuits in a clean plastic bag and bash with a rolling pin. Add the cocoa powder. Melt the butter in a pan and stir in the crumb and cocoa mixture. Press into the base of the cake tin firmly with the back of a spoon. Chill in the refrigerator whilst you prepare the filling.

2 Hull the strawberries and cut them in half. Place them in a pan with the sugar and 80ml/2½fl oz/⅓ cup of water, and simmer for about 5 minutes until the fruit is very soft.

3 Pass the strawberries through a sieve or strainer, pressing the fruit down with the back of a spoon until only a thick pulp is left in the sieve. Scrape any fruit purée from the underside of the sieve and add to the fruit syrup. Discard the pulp which is left in the sieve. Add the gelatine to the warm fruit syrup and whisk until dissolved.

4 Break the jelly into cubes and place in a heatproof jug or pitcher. Pour 100ml/3½fl oz/scant ½ cup of boiling water on to the jelly and stir until it has dissolved. Stir the jelly into the strawberry syrup and leave to cool.

5 In a bowl, mix together the cream cheese and cream, then whisk in the cooled strawberry syrup until thick and creamy.

6 Pour the creamy strawberry mixture on top of the biscuit base and leave to chill in the refrigerator for an hour.

7 For the ganache, break the chocolate into pieces and place in a heatproof bowl over a pan of simmering water with the cream and butter. Simmer until the chocolate and butter have melted. Stir to form a thick glossy ganache. Spread the ganache over the top of the cheesecake and chill for a further 2 hours or overnight.

8 To serve, slide a knife around the tin and remove the base and sides on to a serving plate. The cheesecake will keep in the refrigerator for up to 3 days.

This zesty tangy cheesecake makes a perfect dinner party dessert – citrus flavours are so refreshing after a main meal. You can use limes, lemons or oranges in any combination you want. I love using ginger with citrus but if you are not partial to ginger you can substitute digestive biscuits or graham crackers instead.

St. Clements Cheesecake

For a lemon and lime version replace the orange juice with the juice of 2 limes.

SERVES 12
PREPARATION TIME 30 MINUTES, PLUS CHILLING

FOR THE BASE
300g/10oz ginger biscuits or cookies
150g/5oz/1 stick and 2½ tbsp butter, melted

FOR THE CHEESECAKE
300g/10oz good quality lemon curd
500g/1lb 2oz/2½ cups mascarpone cheese
500ml/17fl oz/2 cups crème fraîche
30ml/2 tbsp icing (confectioners') sugar, plus extra for dusting
Zest and juice of 1 small orange and 1 lemon

Equipment: food processor or blender; 23cm/9in round loose-bottomed cake tin or pan, greased and lined

1 Crush the ginger biscuits to fine crumbs in a food processor or blender, or use a rolling pin to crush the biscuits in a clean plastic bag. Stir the melted butter into the biscuit crumbs in a bowl and then press into the base of the prepared tin using the back of a spoon.

2 Spread two thirds of the lemon curd over the biscuit base.

3 In a mixing bowl, whisk together the mascarpone and crème fraîche until smooth. Sift in the icing sugar, add the lemon and orange zest and juice and remaining lemon curd then whisk again. Taste the mixture and add a little more icing sugar if you wish it to be sweeter.

4 Spoon the mixture over the biscuit base and level with a knife or spatula. Chill in the refrigerator for at least 3 hours or until set.

5 To decorate, dust with a little icing sugar and sprinkle over a little grated zest if you wish. Alternatively you could reserve a few spoonfuls of the buttery biscuit crumb mixture and sprinkle that over the top.

Decorate with a little grated citrus zest if you wish.

I find malted milk drinks one of the most comforting "pick me ups" and this pie is perfect for a special treat. A delicious malted biscuit base is covered with a set malted cream and topped with a rich chocolate ganache and everyone's favourite candy, Maltesers.

Malted Cheesecake Pie

SERVES 12
PREPARATION TIME 30 MINUTES,
PLUS CHILLING

FOR THE BASE
250g/9oz malted milk biscuits or cookies
125g/4½oz/1 stick butter, melted

FOR THE CHEESECAKE
3 sheets leaf gelatine (platinum grade)
360g/12¾oz/1½ cups cream cheese
100g/3½oz/½ cup caster (superfine) sugar
250ml/8fl oz/1 cup double (heavy) cream
70g/2½oz/4 tbsp malted milk powder

FOR THE GANACHE TOPPING
100g/3½oz plain (semisweet) chocolate
60ml/2fl oz/¼ cup double (heavy) cream
28g/1oz/2 tbsp butter
15ml/1 tbsp golden (light corn) syrup
100g/3½oz chocolate malt balls,
   such as Maltesers

Equipment: food processor or blender;
*   23cm/9in round loose-bottomed flan tin*
*   or pie pan, greased*

1 For the biscuit base, crush the biscuits to fine crumbs in a food processor or blender, or place the biscuits in a clean plastic bag and bash with a rolling pin. In a bowl stir the melted butter into the crumbs and then press into the base of the tin tightly with the back of a spoon.

Use a fluted flan tin or pie pan for the prettiest effect.

2 For the cheesecake, soak the gelatine leaves in water until they are soft. Whisk the cream cheese and sugar together until light and creamy. Place the cream in a pan and warm gently. Squeeze the water out of the gelatine leaves and stir into the warm cream (removed from the heat) until the gelatine has dissolved.

3 Pass through a sieve or strainer to remove any undissolved gelatine pieces, then stir in the malted milk powder and whisk well. Carefully add the malted cream to the cream cheese mixture and beat until everything is incorporated. Pour the mixture over the biscuit base and chill in the refrigerator for about 2 hours until the cheesecake is set.

4 For the ganache topping, place the chocolate, cream and butter in a bowl over a pan of simmering water and stir until the chocolate and butter have melted. Add the golden syrup and stir again until glossy.

5 Remove from the heat and leave to cool for a few minutes then gently spread over the top of the cheesecake.

6 Decorate with the chocolate malt balls (either chopped or whole) and return to the refrigerator for another hour until the ganache is set. The cheesecake will keep in the refrigerator for up to 3 days.

Chocolate, bananas and praline walnuts – are there many better combinations? Certainly not if you are a lover of bananas. It is important to use ripe bananas in this recipe for full flavour. This cheesecake is also delicious with pecans or Brazil nuts in place of the walnuts, or a mixture of all three for a nut-a-licious dessert.

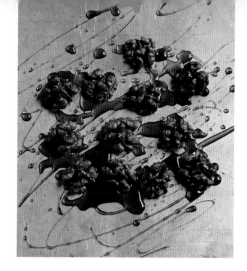

Banana Walnut Chocolate Cheesecake

SERVES: 10
PREPARATION TIME 30 MINUTES, PLUS CHILLING

FOR THE WALNUT PRALINE AND DECORATION
100g/3½oz/½ cup caster (superfine) sugar
100g/3½oz/1 cup walnut halves
200ml/7fl oz/⅔ cup double (heavy) cream

FOR THE BISCUIT CASE
300g/10oz Oreo or similar chocolate cookies
125g/4oz/1 stick butter

FOR THE CHEESECAKE
425ml/14fl oz/1⅔ cups double (heavy) cream
5ml/1 tsp ground cinnamon
5 sheets leaf gelatine (platinum grade)
2 ripe bananas
Juice of 1 lemon
500g/1lb 2oz/2 cups cream cheese

FOR THE CHOCOLATE SAUCE
250ml/8fl oz/1 cup double (heavy) cream
100g/3½oz/7 tbsp butter
150g/5oz plain (semisweet) chocolate
30ml/2 tbsp golden (light corn) syrup

Equipment: silicone mat or greased baking sheet; food processor or blender; 23cm/9in loose-bottomed round springform cake tin or pan, greased and lined; piping or pastry bag fitted with a large star nozzle

1 Begin by preparing the walnut praline. Heat the sugar in a pan until melted and lightly golden brown. Take care towards the end of cooking as the caramel can burn quickly. Do not stir the pan as the sugar is cooking but swirl it to ensure that the sugar does not burn.

2 Spread the walnuts out on a silicone mat or greased baking sheet, mostly in a flat layer – place around 10–12 individually as these will be used to decorate the top of the cheesecake. Using a spoon or fork drizzle swirls of the caramel over the individual walnuts in pretty patterns, then carefully pour the remaining caramel over the rest of the walnuts.

3 Once cool put the individual walnut decorations into an airtight container and blitz the larger walnut praline in a food processor or blender to very fine crumbs.

4 Crush the Oreo cookies to fine crumbs in a food processor or use a rolling pin to crush the biscuits in a clean plastic bag. Melt the butter in a pan over the heat. Stir the biscuit crumbs into the melted butter.

5 Press the biscuit crumb mixture into the base and sides of the prepared tin using the back of a spoon. You want the crumbs to come about 2.5cm/1in up the sides of the tin.

6 For the filling, heat the cream and cinnamon in a pan until warm. Soak the gelatine leaves in water until they are soft, then squeeze out the water. Add the gelatine to the warm cream and stir the mixture until the gelatine has dissolved. Pass the mixture through a fine mesh sieve or strainer.

7 Wrap the tin in clear film or plastic wrap to ensure that there are no leaks. Peel the bananas and discard the skins. In a mixing bowl, whisk the bananas, lemon juice and walnut praline powder together until you have a smooth purée. Add the cream cheese and whisk again, then whisk in the cinnamon cream mixture. Pour the cheesecake filling into the biscuit case. Chill the cheesecake in the refrigerator for at least 3 hours or overnight.

8 To make the chocolate sauce simmer the cream, butter, chocolate and syrup in a pan over a gentle heat until the butter and chocolate have melted. Allow to cool slightly.

9 For the decoration, whisk the cream to stiff peaks in a clean bowl and then spoon into the piping bag. Pipe stars of cream around the edge of the cheesecake and top with the whole caramelized walnut decorations. Serve the cheesecake with the warm chocolate sauce drizzled over. This cheesecake will store for up to 3 days in the refrigerator.

This vibrant green pistachio cheesecake is sweetened with white chocolate and nestled in a bitter chocolate base. The best type of pistachio nuts to use are pistachio nibs which are bright green – often found in Turkish and Iranian supermarkets. I always stock up when I find them as they make any dessert look pretty.

White Chocolate and Pistachio Cheesecake

SERVES 12
PREPARATION TIME 30 MINUTES,
PLUS CHILLING

FOR THE BASE
250g/9oz Oreo cookies or chocolate biscuits
125g/4oz/1 stick butter, melted

FOR THE PISTACHIO PASTE
200g/7oz/1½ cups pistachio nuts
15ml/1 tbsp icing (confectioners') sugar
15–30ml/1–2 tbsp flavourless oil, such as
   vegetable or sunflower oil

FOR THE CHEESECAKE
3 sheets leaf gelatine (platinum grade)
300g/10oz/1½ cups mascarpone cheese
250ml/8fl oz/1 cup double (heavy) cream
150g/5¼oz white chocolate, chopped

Equipment: food processor or blender;
   23cm/9in round loose-bottomed flan tin
   or pie pan, greased

1 For the base, crush the Oreo cookies to fine crumbs in a food processor or blender, or place the cookies in a clean plastic bag and bash with a rolling pin. In a bowl stir the melted butter into the crumbs and then press into the base of the tin tightly with the back of a spoon.

2 Reserve a small handful of pistachio nuts for decoration and place the rest with the icing sugar in a food processor or blender with 15ml/1 tbsp of the oil. Blitz until the nuts are very fine and you have a thick paste. If the mixture is too dry, add a little more oil and blitz again.

3 For the cheesecake, soak the gelatine leaves in water until they are soft. Whisk the mascarpone cheese and pistachio nut paste together until light and creamy.

4 Place the cream in a pan and warm gently. Squeeze the water out of the gelatine leaves and stir into the warm cream (removed from the heat) until the gelatine has dissolved.

5 Pass this mixture through a sieve or strainer to remove any undissolved gelatine, then add 100g/3¼oz of the chopped white chocolate to the warm cream and whisk until melted.

6 Pour the cream into the pistachio mixture and whisk together. Pour the filling on to the base. Finely chop the reserved pistachio nuts and sprinkle over the top of the cheesecake with the remaining chopped white chocolate.

7 Leave to set in the refrigerator for 3 hours or overnight before serving. The cheesecake will keep in the refrigerator for up to 3 days.

This cheesecake is everything a coffee lover could ever want – a coffee biscuit base, creamy coffee caramel cheesecake and swirls of rich mocha ganache. It gives a wonderful caffeine hit and makes a scrumptious dinner party dessert. If you cannot find iced coffee biscuits, just substitute plain biscuits such as rich tea, digestives or graham crackers.

Mocha Cheesecake

SERVES 12
PREPARATION TIME 30 MINUTES, PLUS CHILLING

FOR THE BASE
250g/9oz iced coffee biscuits or cookies
115g/4oz/1 stick butter

FOR THE COFFEE CARAMEL
100g/3½oz/½ cup caster (superfine) sugar
125ml/4fl oz/½ cup espresso coffee
Pinch of salt
300ml/½ pint/1¼ cups double (heavy) cream

FOR THE CHEESECAKE FILLING
5 sheets leaf gelatine (platinum grade)
150g/5oz/¾ cups mascarpone cheese
360g/12¾oz/1½ cups cream cheese

FOR THE MOCHA SWIRLS
100g/3½oz coffee-flavoured plain (semisweet) chocolate, chopped
80ml/2½fl oz/⅓ cup double (heavy) cream
15ml/1 tbsp golden (light corn) syrup
15g/½oz/1 tbsp butter

Equipment: food processor or blender; 23cm/9in loose-bottomed round cake tin or pan, greased and lined

1 Crush the coffee biscuits to fine crumbs in a food processor or blender, or use a rolling pin to crush the biscuits in a clean plastic bag. Melt the butter in a pan over a gentle heat. Stir the biscuit crumbs into the melted butter and then press into the base of the prepared tin using the back of a spoon.

2 Next prepare the coffee caramel. Heat the sugar in a pan over a gentle heat until it has melted. The sugar will start to turn golden brown. Swirl the

pan carefully to ensure that the mixture does not burn. Add the coffee, salt and cream to the pan and stir well to make a caramel. Do not worry if any sugar crystals form as these will melt as you whisk over the heat. Remove from the heat and leave aside to cool slightly.

3 Soak the gelatine leaves in water until they are soft, squeeze out the water, then add to the warm caramel and stir the mixture until the gelatine has dissolved. Pass the mixture through a fine mesh sieve or strainer.

4 In a mixing bowl, whisk together the mascarpone, cream cheese and coffee caramel until smooth. Pour the mixture over the biscuit base.

5 For the mocha swirls, heat the chocolate, cream, syrup and butter in a bowl resting over a pan of water, until melted. Stir everything well so that you have a runny ganache. Leave the mixture to cool slightly then swirl in large patterns over the top of the cheesecake. Using a knife drag the ganache through the cheesecake mixture to swirl.

6 Chill in the refrigerator for at least 3 hours or until set. This cheesecake will store for up to 3 days in the refrigerator.

Coffee and chocolate are a match made in heaven.

Lemon and caramel is perhaps not an obvious flavour combination but it is one that I adore – the sharpness of the lemon cuts through the buttery caramel making this one of my all-time favourite cheesecakes. For an extra indulgent treat, the cheesecake is served with a toffee sauce to drizzle – perfect for cosy dinner parties.

Lemon Caramel Cheesecake

SERVES 12
PREPARATION TIME 30 MINUTES,
PLUS CHILLING

FOR THE CARAMEL
125ml/4fl oz/½ cup sweetened
  condensed milk
50g/1¾oz/3½ tbsp butter
Pinch of salt
125ml/4fl oz/½ cup double (heavy) cream

FOR THE BISCUIT CASE
250g/9oz caramel biscuits or cookies,
  such as Lotus
125g/4½oz/1 stick butter, melted

FOR THE CHEESECAKE
250g/9oz mascarpone cheese
300ml/½ pint/scant 1¼ cups crème fraîche
Juice and zest of 1 lemon
15ml/1 tbsp icing (confectioners') sugar

FOR THE TOFFEE SAUCE
115g/4oz/½ cup light brown sugar
250ml/8fl oz/1 cup double (heavy) cream
50g/1¾oz/3½ tbsp butter

Equipment: food processor or blender;
  23cm/9in round loose-bottomed shallow
  flan tin or pie pan, greased

If you cannot find caramel biscuits use digestives or graham crackers instead.

1 Begin by preparing the caramel. In a heavy pan, heat the condensed milk and butter, whisking all the time until the caramel turns golden brown. Take care that the mixture does not burn. Add the salt and cream, whisking over the heat until the caramel is thick. Remove from the heat, set aside and leave to cool.

2 For the biscuit case, crush the biscuits to fine crumbs in a food processor or blender, or place in a clean plastic bag and bash with a rolling pin. Stir the crumbs into the melted butter and then press the mixture into the base and sides of the tin tightly with the back of a spoon.

3 For the filling, whisk the mascarpone cheese and crème fraîche with the lemon juice, zest and icing sugar.

4 Fold two thirds of the caramel into the mascarpone mixture and spoon into the biscuit case. Drizzle the remaining caramel over the top of the pie and fold in lightly using a spoon to give a rippled effect. Leave to set in the refrigerator for 3 hours or overnight before serving.

5 Just before you are ready to serve, place all the toffee sauce ingredients together in a pan and whisk over a gentle heat until the butter has melted and the sugar dissolved. The sauce should be smooth and thick. Leave to cool slightly. Serve slices of the cheesecake with the warm toffee sauce.

6 The cheesecake will keep in the refrigerator for up to 3 days.

Although peanut brittle is found regularly to buy, I love to make my own almond brittle using whole blanched almonds. It has a buttery, salty taste and makes a perfect topping for this cheesecake. The cheesecake filling is made with almond butter, similar to peanut butter and available from health food shops or in most supermarkets. The recipe makes more almond brittle than you need but it stores well in an airtight container and makes a great sweet snack.

Almond Brittle Cheesecake

SERVES 12
PREPARATION TIME 30 MINUTES,
PLUS CHILLING

FOR THE BISCUIT CASE
250g/9oz amarettini or amaretti
125g/4½oz/1 stick butter, melted

FOR THE CHEESECAKE
3 sheets leaf gelatine (platinum grade)
250g/9oz ricotta cheese
125g/4¼oz/½ cup cream cheese
50g/1¾oz/¼ cup caster (superfine) sugar
50g/1¾oz/scant ¼ cup soft light
   brown sugar
45ml/3 tbsp almond butter
250ml/8fl oz/1 cup double (heavy) cream

FOR THE ALMOND BRITTLE
200g/7oz/1 cup caster (superfine) sugar
80ml/2½fl oz/⅓ cup golden (light
   corn) syrup
150g/5oz whole blanched almonds
45ml/3 tbsp almond butter
2.5ml/½ tsp salt
50g/1¾oz/3½ tbsp salted butter
5ml/1 tsp bicarbonate of soda (baking soda)

*Equipment: food processor or blender;
   sugar thermometer; silicone mat or
   greased baking sheet; 23cm/9in round
   loose-bottomed cake tin or pan, greased*

1 For the biscuit case, crush the amarettini to fine crumbs in a food processor or blender, or place the biscuits in a clean plastic bag and bash with a rolling pin. Stir the melted butter into the crumbs in a bowl and then press into the base and sides of the tin tightly with the back of a spoon.

2 For the cheesecake, soak the gelatine leaves in water until they are soft. Whisk the ricotta and cream cheeses together with the two sugars and almond butter until light and creamy. Place the cream in a pan and warm gently.

3 Squeeze the water out of the gelatine leaves and stir into the warm cream, removed from the heat, until the gelatine has dissolved. Pass through a sieve or strainer.

4 Leave to cool slightly then pour the cream into the almond mixture and whisk together. Pour the filling into the biscuit case. Leave to set in the refrigerator for 3 hours or overnight.

5 For the almond brittle, heat the sugar, syrup and 45ml/3 tbsp water in a pan until the sugar has melted, then bring to the boil until the temperature reaches 138°C/280°F (hard ball stage). It is best to use a sugar thermometer for this to measure the temperature accurately but if you do not have one, boil the sugar for about 5 minutes then drop a small amount of the liquid carefully into a glass of cold water. If the mixture forms into a ball that is solid when you remove it from the glass, the mixture is ready.

6 Add the almonds, almond butter, salt and butter to the pan and beat well. The mixture will become stiff. Beat in the bicarbonate of soda.

7 Quickly tip the mixture on to the silicone mat or greased baking sheet, taking care as the mixture will be very hot. Spread the mixture out into a layer about 1cm/½in in thickness using a spatula and leave to cool. When the brittle is cold you can break it into small pieces using your hands or a rolling pin. Sprinkle some of the brittle over the top of the cheesecake to decorate. The cheesecake will keep in the refrigerator for up to 3 days.

Nutritional Notes

Peanut Butter and Cashew Squares (makes 24) Energy 191kcal/802kJ; Protein 2.8g; Carbohydrate 24.2g, of which sugars 14.1g; Fat 10g, of which saturates 4.9g; Cholesterol 11mg; Calcium 64mg; Fibre 0.4g; Sodium 99mg.

Pink and White Marshmallow Crispy Cakes (makes 14) Energy 192kcal/810kJ; Protein 1.7g; Carbohydrate 31.5g, of which sugars 17g; Fat 7.5g, of which saturates 4.7g; Cholesterol 19mg; Calcium 58mg; Fibre 0.2g; Sodium 140mg.

Black and White Rice Crispy Slices (makes 32) Energy 194kcal/815kJ; Protein 2.4g; Carbohydrate 28.2g, of which sugars 20.7g; Fat 8.8g, of which saturates 5.3g; Cholesterol 8mg; Calcium 70mg; Fibre 0.3g; Sodium 79mg.

Salted Caramel Cornflake Cakes (makes 15) Energy 241kcal/1013kJ; Protein 1.9g; Carbohydrate 35.6g, of which sugars 21.1g; Fat 11.1g, of which saturates 7g; Cholesterol 28mg; Calcium 5mg; Fibre 0.4g; Sodium 220mg.

Malted Chocolate Crispy Cakes (makes 20) Energy 135kcal/570kJ; Protein 1.7g; Carbohydrate 24.9g, of which sugars 15.7g; Fat 4.2g, of which saturates 2.2g; Cholesterol 7mg; Calcium 41mg; Fibre 0.6g; Sodium 158mg.

Hazelnut Praline Squares (makes 16) Energy 206kcal/863kJ; Protein 2.3g; Carbohydrate 22.6g, of which sugars 14.6g; Fat 12.5g, of which saturates 4.7g; Cholesterol 13mg; Calcium 52mg; Fibre 1g; Sodium 92mg.

Coconut Popping Candy Cakes (makes 24) Energy 191kcal/801kJ; Protein 1.9g; Carbohydrate 24.8g, of which sugars 14.7g; Fat 10g, of which saturates 7.7g; Cholesterol 8mg; Calcium 48mg; Fibre 0.9g; Sodium 88mg.

Caramel Crispy Nests (makes 12) Energy 350kcal/1462kJ; Protein 4.1g; Carbohydrate 39.2g, of which sugars 25.7g; Fat 20.7g, of which saturates 12.5g; Cholesterol 34mg; Calcium 67mg; Fibre 2.2g; Sodium 133mg.

Sweet and Salty After-party Tiffin (makes 25) Energy 195kcal/812kJ; Protein 1.5g; Carbohydrate 19g, of which sugars 13.3g; Fat 13g, of which saturates 7.4g; Cholesterol 18mg; Calcium 10mg; Fibre 0.7g; Sodium 153mg.

S'Mores Bites (makes 16) Energy 169kcal/707kJ; Protein 1.4g; Carbohydrate 18.9g, of which sugars 13.5g; Fat 10.3g, of which saturates 6.1g; Cholesterol 17mg; Calcium 13mg; Fibre 0.4g; Sodium 94mg.

Oreo Cookie Garden Cakes (makes 16) Energy 388kcal/1623kJ; Protein 3g; Carbohydrate 42.3g, of which sugars 38.3g; Fat 24.2g, of which saturates 14.7g; Cholesterol 30mg; Calcium 40mg; Fibre 1.2g; Sodium 130mg.

Black Forest Slice (makes 30) Energy 204kcal/854kJ; Protein 1.7g; Carbohydrate 22.9g, of which sugars 17.2g; Fat 12.4g, of which saturates 7.3g; Cholesterol 22mg; Calcium 21mg; Fibre 0.5g; Sodium 114mg.

Chocolate Peppermint Slice (makes 20) Energy 248kcal/1037kJ; Protein 1.7g; Carbohydrate 27.6g, of which sugars 21.7g; Fat 15.4g, of which saturates 9.2g; Cholesterol 31mg; Calcium 21mg; Fibre 0.3g; Sodium 123mg.

Ginger Truffle Squares (makes 16) Energy 266kcal/1107kJ; Protein 1.9g; Carbohydrate 23.3g, of which sugars 15.9g; Fat 19g, of which saturates 11.7g; Cholesterol 36mg; Calcium 33mg; Fibre 0.4g; Sodium 137mg.

Christmas Pudding Tiffin (serves 14) Energy 366kcal/1532kJ; Protein 2.6g; Carbohydrate 46.4g, of which sugars 38.6g; Fat 19.6g, of which saturates 11.8g; Cholesterol 30mg; Calcium 46mg; Fibre 0.8g; Sodium 158mg.

Salame di Cioccolato (20 slices) Energy 162kcal/674kJ; Protein 1.9g; Carbohydrate 11.5g, of which sugars 8.5g; Fat 12.1g, of which saturates 6.1g; Cholesterol 36mg; Calcium 16mg; Fibre 0.7g; Sodium 91mg.

Eton Mess Layer Dessert (serves 8) Energy 457kcal/1894kJ; Protein 2.8g; Carbohydrate 21.9g, of which sugars 21.9g; Fat 40.4g, of which saturates 25.1g; Cholesterol 103mg; Calcium 56mg; Fibre 2g; Sodium 36mg.

Crispy Fresh Berry Layer Cake (serves 8) Energy 440kcal/1837kJ; Protein 3.8g; Carbohydrate 46g, of which sugars 30.4g; Fat 28.1g, of which saturates 17.4g; Cholesterol 64mg; Calcium 111mg; Fibre 0.9g; Sodium 157mg.

Peanut Chocolate Fudge Cake (serves 12) Energy 534kcal/2210kJ; Protein 10.3g; Carbohydrate 21.7g, of which sugars 16.6g; Fat 49.2g, of which saturates 25.4g; Cholesterol 87mg; Calcium 76mg; Fibre 1.7g; Sodium 297mg.

White Chocolate and Blueberry Layer Cake (serves 12) Energy 293kcal/1224kJ; Protein 4.3g; Carbohydrate 30g, of which sugars 21.3g; Fat 18.3g, of which saturates 8.7g; Cholesterol 24mg; Calcium 65mg; Fibre 1.5g; Sodium 152mg.

Salted Honey and Apricot Flan (serves 8) Energy 481kcal/2001kJ; Protein 6.3g; Carbohydrate 36.2g, of which sugars 29.1g; Fat 35.6g, of which saturates 20.2g; Cholesterol 159mg; Calcium 84mg; Fibre 2.5g; Sodium 130mg.

Rum and Raisin Brownie Torte (serves 16) Energy 306kcal/1272kJ; Protein 3.3g; Carbohydrate 24.3g, of which sugars 23.4g; Fat 21.1g, of which saturates 12.8g; Cholesterol 69mg; Calcium 38mg; Fibre 1.2g; Sodium 47mg.

Pineapple and Coffee Truffle Cake (serves 12) Energy 540kcal/2250kJ; Protein 5.3g; Carbohydrate 43.6g, of which sugars 34.4g; Fat 37.7g, of which saturates 22.5g; Cholesterol 104mg; Calcium 76mg; Fibre 0.8g; Sodium 165mg.

Cinnamon Pretzel Crunchie Cake (serves 12) Energy 677kcal/2809kJ; Protein 5.7g; Carbohydrate 39.9g, of which sugars 25.1g; Fat 55.9g, of which saturates 34g; Cholesterol 159mg; Calcium 80mg; Fibre 0.5g; Sodium 464mg.

Sour Cherry Ice Cream Bombe (serves 10) Energy 424kcal/1773kJ; Protein 5.2g; Carbohydrate 42.8g, of which sugars 37.7g; Fat 27g, of which saturates 15.8g; Cholesterol 81mg; Calcium 147mg; Fibre 0.6g; Sodium 134mg.

Neopolitan Cookie Crumb Towers (serves 6) Energy 683kcal/2853kJ; Protein 8.8g; Carbohydrate 73.2g, of which sugars 53g; Fat 41.4g, of which saturates 25.6g; Cholesterol 101mg; Calcium 227mg; Fibre 0g; Sodium 408mg.

Jelly and Ice Cream Cake (serves 10) Energy 500kcal/2109kJ; Protein 10g; Carbohydrate 84.3g, of which sugars 82.3g; Fat 16.1g, of which saturates 10.4g; Cholesterol 52mg; Calcium 241mg; Fibre 0.7g; Sodium 134mg.

Peanut Butter Ice Cream Cake (serves 10) Energy 513kcal/2124kJ; Protein 9.7g; Carbohydrate 21.9g, of which sugars 19.7g; Fat 45.6g, of which saturates 22.8g; Cholesterol 78mg; Calcium 90mg; Fibre 1.3g; Sodium 306mg.

Blueberry Streusel Ice Cream Cake (serves 8) Energy 528kcal/2208kJ; Protein 5.5g; Carbohydrate 62.8g, of which sugars 45.5g; Fat 30.3g, of which saturates 11.4g; Cholesterol 12mg; Calcium 89mg; Fibre 3g; Sodium 224mg.

Coconut Honey Ice Cream Bombe (serves 10) Energy 350kcal/1458kJ; Protein 4.4g; Carbohydrate 27.7g, of which sugars 27.5g; Fat 25.4g, of which saturates 15.6g; Cholesterol 133mg; Calcium 84mg; Fibre 1.3g; Sodium 76mg.

Toffee Apple Ice Cream Pie (serves 10) Energy 609kcal/2548kJ; Protein 6.3g; Carbohydrate 71.6g, of which sugars 57.5g; Fat 35g, of which saturates 21.3g; Cholesterol 79mg; Calcium 165mg; Fibre 2.2g; Sodium 275mg.

KitKat Ice Cream Cake (serves 10) Energy 643kcal/2695kJ; Protein 9.2g; Carbohydrate 76.7g, of which sugars 63.9g; Fat 35.4g, of which saturates 21.6g; Cholesterol 59mg; Calcium 237mg; Fibre 0g; Sodium 240mg.

Strawberry Jelly Cheesecake (serves 12) Energy 557kcal/2319kJ; Protein 5g; Carbohydrate 49.1g, of which sugars 34.9g; Fat 39.2g, of which saturates 23.5g; Cholesterol 81mg; Calcium 81mg; Fibre 1.6g; Sodium 318mg.

St Clements Cheesecake (serves 12) Energy 523kcal/2176kJ; Protein 6.6g; Carbohydrate 40.6g, of which sugars 22.6g; Fat 38.2g, of which saturates 24.1g; Cholesterol 99mg; Calcium 103mg; Fibre 0g; Sodium 328mg.

Malted Cheesecake Pie (serves 12) Energy 577kcal/2399kJ; Protein 3.8g; Carbohydrate 40.6g, of which sugars 27.6g; Fat 45.9g, of which saturates 27.5g; Cholesterol 101mg; Calcium 105mg; Fibre 0.6g; Sodium 332mg.

Banana Walnut Chocolate Cheesecake (serves 10) Energy 1180kcal/4882kJ; Protein 7.6g; Carbohydrate 48.4g, of which sugars 36.4g; Fat 107.5g, of which saturates 62.7g; Cholesterol 232mg; Calcium 140mg; Fibre 1.2g; Sodium 451mg.

White Chocolate and Pistachio Cheesecake (serves 12) Energy 505kcal/2094kJ; Protein 8.3g; Carbohydrate 25.1g, of which sugars 15.9g; Fat 41.9g, of which saturates 21.1g; Cholesterol 73mg; Calcium 107mg; Fibre 1.4g; Sodium 350mg.

Mocha Cheesecake (serves 12) Energy 551kcal/2287kJ; Protein 4g; Carbohydrate 31.2g, of which sugars 26.2g; Fat 46.5g, of which saturates 29g; Cholesterol 114mg; Calcium 92mg; Fibre 0.5g; Sodium 251mg.

Lemon Caramel Cheesecake (serves 12) Energy 599kcal/2485kJ; Protein 5.3g; Carbohydrate 35.6g, of which sugars 25.7g; Fat 49.4g, of which saturates 31.1g; Cholesterol 125mg; Calcium 114mg; Fibre 0g; Sodium 282mg.

Almond Brittle Cheesecake (serves 12) Energy 638kcal/2661kJ; Protein 8.5g; Carbohydrate 51.8g, of which sugars 39.9g; Fat 46g, of which saturates 22.2g; Cholesterol 80mg; Calcium 104mg; Fibre 1.4g; Sodium 286mg.

Index

INDEX

This edition is published by Lorenz Books,
an imprint of Anness Publishing Ltd, 108 Great Russell Street,
London WC1B 3NA; info@anness.com

www.lorenzbooks.com; www.annesspublishing.com;
twitter: @Anness_Books

If you like the images in this book and would like to investigate using
them for publishing, promotions or advertising, please visit our website
www.practicalpictures.com for more information.

© Anness Publishing Ltd 2016

A CIP catalogue record for this book is available from
the British Library.

Publisher: Joanna Lorenz
Photographer, Prop Stylist and Designer: Steve Painter
Food Stylist: Lucy Mckelvie
Editorial: Sarah Lumby

COOK'S NOTES
Bracketed terms are intended for American readers.
For all recipes, quantities are given in both metric and imperial measures
and, where appropriate, in standard cups and spoons. Follow one set of
measures, but not a mixture, because they are not interchangeable.
Standard spoon and cup measures are level.
1 tsp = 5ml, 1 tbsp = 15ml, 1 cup = 250ml/8fl oz.
Australian standard tablespoons are 20ml. Australian readers should use
3 tsp in place of 1 tbsp for measuring small quantities. American pints are
16fl oz/2 cups. American readers should use 20fl oz/2.5 cups in place of
1 pint when measuring liquids.
The nutritional analysis given for each recipe is calculated per portion
(i.e. serving or item), unless otherwise stated. If the recipe gives a range,
such as Serves 4–6, then the nutritional analysis will be for the smaller
portion size, i.e. 6 servings. The analysis does not include optional
ingredients, such as salt added to taste.
Medium (US large) eggs are used unless otherwise stated.

PUBLISHER'S NOTE
Although the advice and information in this book are believed to be
accurate and true at the time of going to press, neither the authors nor
the publisher can accept any legal responsibility or liability for any errors
or omissions that may have been made nor for any inaccuracies nor for
any loss, harm or injury that comes about from following instructions or
advice in this book.